H. Merchant
New York
8/31/44

FOR DOROTHY PARKER

The Searching Wind

A PLAY IN TWO ACTS

BY LILLIAN HELLMAN

NEW YORK : THE VIKING PRESS : MCMXLIV

THIS EDITION IS PRODUCED IN FULL COMPLIANCE WITH
ALL WAR PRODUCTION BOARD CONSERVATION ORDERS

FIRST PUBLISHED BY THE VIKING PRESS IN JUNE 1944

PUBLISHED ON THE SAME DAY IN THE DOMINION OF CANADA
BY THE MACMILLAN COMPANY OF CANADA LIMITED

PRINTED IN U. S. A. BY THE COLONIAL PRESS

HERMAN SHUMLIN PRESENTS
LILLIAN HELLMAN'S NEW PLAY

The Searching Wind

CAST

(IN ORDER OF THEIR APPEARANCE)

MOSES TANEY	Dudley Digges
SAMUEL HAZEN	Montgomery Clift
PONETTE	Alfred Hesse
SOPHRONIA	Mercedes Gilbert
EMILY HAZEN	Cornelia Otis Skinner
ALEXANDER HAZEN	Dennis King
CATHERINE BOWMAN	Barbara O'Neil
ELDERLY ITALIAN WAITER	Edgar Andrews
YOUNG ITALIAN WAITER	Joseph de Santis
MANAGER OF THE GRAND HOTEL	Walter Kohler
EPPLER	William F. Schoeller
EDWARD HALSEY	Eric Latham
JAMES SEARS	Eugene Earl
COUNT MAX VON STAMMER	Arnold Korff

Soldiers, restaurant guests, waiters, people in the street

Opened at the Fulton Theatre on the night of April 12, 1944.

Synopsis of Scenes

ACT ONE

ACT TWO

Act One: Scene 1

The drawing room of the Hazen house is a room of fine proportions with good furniture, good pictures, and good ornaments. Right stage is a large arch leading to an entrance hall; left stage are French doors which open on a terrace; right center stage is a door leading to a hall off which are the dining room and kitchen quarters. Downstage, left, are a chair and a table. A small couch is center stage. Upstage, right, is a piano; downstage, right, a large couch and a chair. Books and magazines are piled on the tables. The doors leading to the terrace are open; two chairs are on the terrace, a table between them. Throughout the play stage directions "left" and "right" are the audience's left and right.

As the curtain rises, Moses Taney, a man of about seventy, is sitting in a large chair. He is in dinner clothes and he is reading a newspaper. Corporal Samuel Hazen, a pleasant-looking young man of twenty, is sitting on the small couch, his right leg propped up on a chair. He, too, is reading a newspaper. Near the couch is a heavy cane.

MOSES *puts his paper down, looks at Sam:* What do you think of it, Sam?

SAM *without looking up:* I don't know, Grandpa. I don't read as fast as you do. I still have to spell out the words.

7

MOSES *smiles, nods:* I know. Must be hard to learn to read in only one year at Harvard. If your international mother and father hadn't taught you so many other languages— I don't believe in teaching Americans other languages. We never really learn them. Only the fancy words in which to gossip, or eat, or be malicious. Hey, Sam, answer me.

SAM: Shut up, Grandpa, and let me read.

MOSES *after a second, yawns, then picks up the newspaper:* Maybe it would be quicker if I read it to you. *Begins to read:* "This is the first of a series of articles by former Ambassador Alexander Hazen. Mr. Hazen has just returned from a tour of Africa and Southern Italy. Although Mr. Hazen has never before been willing to write his impressions of the current scene, this newspaper convinced him that although—" What in hell do they think "although" means? People on newspapers write English as if a rat were caught in the typewriter and they were trying to hit the keys which wouldn't disturb it.

SAM *laughs:* All right, Grandpa. I'll read Father's article after you go to bed.

MOSES: Why do you have to read it twice? In three thousand words of diplomatic double talk it says that sometimes democracies have to deal with people they don't approve and sometimes, in order to save something or other, you have to do something else or other. It's simple.

SAM *laughs:* It's not simple to me.

MOSES: Why?

SAM *a little uncomfortably:* Oh, I'm nobody to judge. What did I see of Italy? The people in a little town, a river, some hills, a hospital. Father is an important man, he saw important people. I was just a soldier, I—

MOSES: Does that make you less capable of thinking?

SAM *smiles:* Now don't give me lecture six on thinking for myself. I'm trying. I'm slow at it. *Points to Moses.* Children of famous fathers and famous grandfathers learn to walk late. I used to tell that to my friend Leck.

MOSES: Does your friend Leck think, or does he come from a famous father?

SAM: He was a good thinker. His father was a baker in Jersey City and so was Leck. He's dead, Grandpa, and I told you that once before.

MOSES *eagerly, worried:* Sorry, sorry, Sam. At my age you forget what's important and—

SAM: I liked Leck.

MOSES: —and remember what isn't. *Points to the newspaper.* I can almost remember the words in which your father and I talked about this same Victor Emmanuel gentleman twenty-two years ago, the day Mussolini marched into Rome. *Waves the paper.* I ran the paper then— *As he speaks the hall door opens and a tall Frenchman of about forty-five comes in carrying a tray on which are bottles, glasses, soda. He is in butler's uniform but it does not look well on him. He slowly crosses the room, bows to Moses and Sam, goes out into the entrance hall.*

SAM: Where's he going with that?

MOSES: I've come to think it's best not to ask him. Tonight he seems headed for the garage.

SAM *points to the paper:* Grandpa, why did you ever sell the paper? Everybody says it used to be so good, and now it's nothing. It's just wishy-washy when it's not downright bad.

MOSES: I didn't sell it. I never could have sold it. It was that way in my father's will. I leased it to them.

SAM *after a second:* How could you let them make it into anything like this? I'd always thought you sold it, needed the money or something—

MOSES: I don't read it often. I advise you not to.

SAM *frowns:* Don't you care? How could you have given it up? Let it become this?—

MOSES: It's a long story, son. Like all former thinkers, I'm writing a book. Or rather I keep a book. It's meant for you to read.

SAM: I'll have plenty of time to read it. I think they'll discharge me soon.

MOSES *quickly, nervously:* Discharge you? Why should they do that? You told us Roberts said your leg—

SAM *quickly:* I just think they will. I don't know what I'll do with myself after two years of the army.

MOSES: Go sit in the library and read. You smile, but that would be a serious thing to do and you're going to be a serious man. If I'm wrong and you're not serious, I'll give you the newspaper and you can spend the rest of your life acting important and misinforming folks. That would break my heart, Sam.

Ponette reappears with the tray. He moves to the table near Sam, starts to put the tray on it, changes his mind, moves toward a very small table, puts down the tray, catches it as it totters. Then he moves toward the large table, puts the tray on it. Turns, sees that Moses and Sam are staring at him.

PONETTE *in a heavy French accent:* Pardon. You think that Madame Hazen tonight wishes here, or table terrace?

SAM *pleasantly:* It doesn't matter. Put it any place.

Ponette stares at the tray, decides to push it to other end of table. As he pushes it, a glass falls, doesn't break. He sighs, picks it up, shakes his head.

PONETTE: In my country to drop and not to break is thought to be ill-luckness.

MOSES: In our country it is considered to be awkwardnessism. Don't worry about it, Ponette.

Sophronia, a nice-looking Negro woman of about sixty-two, comes in from the open hall door. She is carrying a rag.

SOPHRONIA: What spilled tonight?

PONETTE *pleased with himself:* Not a drop.

MOSES: It's not spilling night, it's dropping night.

Emily Hazen comes rapidly into the room. She is a handsome woman of about forty-three or four. She has on a dinner dress. She is frowning; she is nervous.

EMILY: Is anything wrong in the kitchen? There's been so much noise.

PONETTE: It is most difficult for a woman like my wife to be a cook. She was a lady at home, such as you, Madame—

SOPHRONIA *sharply:* Yes. Remember, Mr. Taney, how every Southerner came from a family that had been ruined by the Civil War? Now there's never a refugee who wasn't rich.

EMILY *quickly:* All right, Sophronia. *To Ponette, as she runs toward the hall door:* Will you make martinis, please? *He picks up a bottle of scotch.* With gin, please, gin. *She moves out.*

SAM: I've never seen Mother nervous before. What's the matter tonight?

PONETTE *makes a face as he pours the gin:* Ugh. I do not like gin.

MOSES: Then it would be wise not to drink it.

PONETTE *having poured the gin into the pitcher, hesitates:* With soda, Monsieur?

SAM *laughs:* Try it that way. Might be interesting.

SOPHRONIA *impatiently:* Vermouth, vermouth. Three to one.

PONETTE *delighted:* Ah, vermouth. Merci. *Picks up bottle.* Le vermouth de France.

MOSES: He makes it sound as if the vermouth is related to him. *Quickly crosses the room, takes the bottle from Ponette.* Thank you. But let me do it, please.

SOPHRONIA: It is all the fault of the United Front.

PONETTE *as Moses and Sam laugh:* Ah, you gentlemen laugh. But it is not a joke. If it had not been for the radicals of France— *Shrugs*. If it comes in your country, should God forbid, you will see the danger. It is the fault of Léon Blum— Like me, you will lose your store, your beautiful house, your—

MOSES: We have no store. *Ponette shakes his head, exits.*

SAM *to Sophronia:* Why do we have to have people like that in the house? What's he talking about?

SOPHRONIA: He used to have a dry goods store in Toulouse.

MOSES: Some people don't think that's the best training for a butler.

SOPHRONIA *points to the kitchen:* And his wife used to have a servant of her own, and lock the icebox every night and why don't we lock our iceboxes and if it hadn't been for those people who used to go on strikes the Germans would never have come into France and if it hadn't been for their crazy son-in-law who was a Socialist they would never have had to leave. *She moves toward the hall door as Emily re-enters.* Stay out of the kitchen, Miss Emily. I'll watch things. *She exits.*

EMILY *shakes her head:* Sophronia doesn't like our refugees.

MOSES: No old American stock likes that kind of foreigner. We're polite to 'em but we don't like 'em. Narrow of us.

EMILY: Are you dining here?

MOSES: Yes.

EMILY: Oh. *Hesitantly, nervously turns to Sam:* You told me this morning, Sam, you wanted dinner in your room.

SAM: I had to go out this afternoon, so I thought I'd stay up and eat downstairs tonight. I'm tired of bed.

EMILY *turns to look at him:* You had to go out? But the doctor told you not to get up for more than a few hours a day—

SAM *quickly:* I'm all right, Mother. I didn't move around much.

EMILY *warmly:* Please don't do it again, darling. Please do what the doctor tells you. Then in another month you'll be fine.

SAM *turns away, sharply:* All right, Mother.

EMILY *stares at him for a second, then to Moses:* You said you were going to the Hapgoods for dinner.

MOSES: I changed my mind. I want to be with Sam.

EMILY *hesitates:* You see, er—I—er—Catherine Bowman is coming. I haven't seen her in over twenty years and—

MOSES: And you didn't want us here. Then we shall certainly stay. Any dinner at which you are not wanted is always a little less dull than one at which you are.

EMILY: Father, why don't you take an apartment at the Shoreham and have tea with us on Sundays?

SAM *laughs:* I wouldn't like that. I'd miss Grandpa.

MOSES *pleased:* Would you, son? Well, I'm not going. Your mother always forgets this house belongs to me. And when I die, it will belong to you.

EMILY *to Sam:* I wonder what's happened to your father?

I heard him come home an hour ago. *Turns to Moses, as if wishing to talk:* So you're not leaving the house to me?

MOSES: You've got too much money as it is. You and Alex don't need a house. You'll always be busy ambassadoring in Europe, talking away in eight languages, in that diplomatic basic English—*To Emily:* Do stop moving about. You're not a fidgety woman and it doesn't become you. *To Sam:* If *you* turn out to be a diplomat, I'll cut you out of my will.

As he speaks, Alexander Hazen, a good-looking man of about fifty, comes in from the hall. He is in dinner clothes. He smiles at Emily, crosses to Sam, pats him on the arm.

SAM: I'm not going to be a diplomat, but that won't be my reason. *He looks up at Alex, smiles, presses Alex's arm.*

MOSES: Don't be so sure. You come from a long line of men who've meddled in the affairs of this country. Your father's father, for example—

ALEX *smiles:* My father didn't like you either. Sam, Sears told me he saw you going into the hospital this afternoon. I went over immediately, but nobody knew anything about it and Colonel Roberts wasn't there. What's the matter?

EMILY *comes quickly to Sam:* Why didn't you tell me? What did you go to the hospital for?

SAM *pleasantly:* I didn't go to the hospital. Sears was mistaken. *He pats Emily's hand.* Nothing's the matter, Mother.

ALEX: How could Sears have been mistaken?

SAM *quickly, firmly:* He was mistaken, Father. *To Emily:*

Can I have another? *Both Emily and Alex look at him; then Emily takes his glass, moves toward the table.*

ALEX *points to the newspaper:* What did you think of my piece, Sam?

SAM *uncomfortably:* You can't read in a room with Grandpa.

ALEX *pleasantly:* That means you didn't like it.

SAM *very uncomfortably:* There were some things I didn't understand. We didn't see Italy the same way—

ALEX: Then it must be that I saw it wrong. *Smiles.* Funny. I remember my father telling me about France. I kept wanting to say, for God's sake, I fought there: you can't know about it the way I do.

EMILY *moves toward the door:* Is that a taxi coming in? *Shakes her head.* Alex—

ALEX: I had hoped we were dining alone. I've had a tough day. Who's coming?

EMILY: Cassie Bowman. *Very quickly:* Have another cocktail, Father? You've made good martinis—

ALEX *very slowly:* Why is Cassie coming here?

EMILY *brightly, to Sam:* Cassie's never seen you or Sarah, which seems strange to me. Cassie and I grew up together, school and college and down the street, and your grandfather used to take us to Europe in the summer. Your father used to take us both to dances and—

ALEX *who has not moved from the table:* Why is Cassie coming?

EMILY *too lightly:* Why not? You've seen her—when was the last time?—but I haven't in twenty, twenty-one years. Well, it seems it's her sabbatical— *Cheerily, to Sam and Moses:* She's teaching girls the age we were when I last saw her. That makes me feel so old— *To Alex:* She's visiting the Taylors. It seemed crazy, sort of, for Cassie to be in Washington and not to have her here—

ALEX: I saw her—*Slowly*—last week.

EMILY *quickly:* But *I* haven't seen her, Alex.

ALEX: You haven't wanted to. Neither has she. Why to-night?

SAM: Why didn't you see each other, if you were such good friends? A fight?

EMILY *quickly:* No, no. No fight. I don't know why. Or maybe I—

MOSES: No martinis need that much stirring, Alex. Do stop it and pour. *To Emily:* Couldn't you stop fidgeting? *The front door bell rings. Emily immediately turns toward the terrace doors, frowns, turns to face the hall. Alex moves toward the hall, stops.* This can't have the historic importance of the reconciliation of General Grant and General Lee.

Catherine Bowman comes in the door. She is a good-looking woman of about forty-four. She has on a simple dinner dress. Her movements are hesitant, cautious, as if she were unsure of herself. She stands for a minute staring at Emily, then looks at Alex, looks back at Emily.

CASSIE *softly, to Emily:* I wanted to come in by the terrace. The way I used to when we were kids.

EMILY *softly, coming toward her, smiles:* I know. I turned that way, expecting you to come up the terrace steps. *They touch hands. There is an awkward pause, and then Cassie turns to Alex who has come up to her.*

CASSIE *softly:* Hello, Alex.

ALEX *softly:* Cassie.

CASSIE *shakes hands with Moses. Warmly:* Hello, Mr. Taney. It's been a long time.

EMILY: Well. We've finally met again. *To Moses, too brightly:* How do you think Cassie looks, Father, after all those years?

MOSES: Perhaps a little younger than you, if that's what you wanted not to hear.

EMILY *to Cassie:* And this is my son, Sam. Our girl is away at school—

Sam, leaning on his cane, is moving toward Cassie.

CASSIE: I'm glad to know you. Your father has spoken of you so often. *Points to the ribbon on Sam's chest.* Does he tell you how proud he is of that? Your father told me last night that your leg was getting better. I'm so glad to hear that.

Emily moves nervously. Alex turns to the table.

SAM *smiles:* There's too much talk about my leg. You'd think it was the only leg that had been in a war.

EMILY: Do give us a cocktail, Alex. *To Cassie, smiling:* Well. Well. That seems to be all I can say after all these years. *As Alex comes to them with the pitcher, to Cassie:*

Let's have several cocktails quick. They'll help. Don't go away, Alex. We'll swallow this one and you stand by for another. *Cassie laughs, gulps her cocktail.* I'm not used to drinking much, are you?

CASSIE: No, but it might be a good idea tonight.

Emily motions for Alex to pour another. They both drink, both cough.

MOSES *to Sam:* They're going to fall flat on each other's faces.

CASSIE: You used to say that, Mr. Taney.

MOSES *bows:* Cassie, it takes a great woman to remember what I used to say.

CASSIE: Or one who has missed you.

MOSES: As soon as I've had soup, you and I may fall in love.

SAM *laughs:* Don't, Grandpa. You'd keep me awake nights telling me about it.

EMILY *to Cassie:* I want to hear about you, Cassie. How's college and have you liked teaching?

CASSIE: Most of the time.

EMILY *smiles, helplessly:* Oh, come on, Cassie. Help me.

CASSIE: Well. Not much about me. I'm head of the English department now. Everybody's got a specialty, so mine's poetry. The town still looks the same. Old lady Carter in the history department—remember her?—she died and I've got her house and I go down to New York whenever I can and oh, well, I don't know, I see the same people, I take long vacations when I can—

MOSES *shocked:* Didn't you ever get married, Cassie?

CASSIE *very quickly:* No, sir, I didn't. I'm an old maid, I—

MOSES: How'd that happen? You're a good-looking woman—

CASSIE *quickly, to Emily:* It's a small life, mine. Not like yours. It just goes on— *Smiles, lamely.* I guess that's all.

EMILY: All right, then I'll get me over with. We've been abroad most of the time, as you know. I'm sorry I missed you that day in Paris. Well, after '39 Alex stayed on in London as a kind of Ambassador without a country, or maybe with too many countries, the governments-in-exile, I mean—

CASSIE *looks toward Alex, uncomfortably:* I know, Em. I—

EMILY: Although Biddle takes care of them, really, or he did. I came back home last year and Sam went into the army, before that, I mean, and Alex stayed on for a while—

ALEX: Emily—

EMILY: Then Alex went to Italy as an observer—Sam and Alex were there at the same time, but they didn't see each other—and then Sam came back wounded and Alex got back last month. I'm not talking English.

ALEX *carefully:* Em, I've been trying to tell you that Cas knows all that. You've forgotten I've seen her.

EMILY: Oh, you mean at dinner last week, last night. Well, I wanted to bring her up to date. *Helplessly:* It's been so long— We have to start somewhere—

MOSES: Who are we sending over, Alex, to take care of those elderly clowns who call themselves governments-in-exile?

ALEX *sharply:* I don't know. And they're not clowns.

MOSES: Certainly not. Not *all* of them. Only most. Ah, well, our time likes its old men to run the world. In our world we won't let the young run our affairs—

ALEX: Ready with your lecture on Charles James Fox, Moses?

MOSES *as if he hadn't heard him:* We think of young men as fit only for battles and for death.

SAM *leans forward:* Two years ago, Grandpa, I'd have yawned or laughed at that. I can't do either now.

ALEX: That's because it's not funny and it's not true. Those men are doing the best they can. And so are we.

MOSES: So you say in your article. But the fact remains that every old mummy is being preserved: the gentlemen from Poland, the gentlemen from Italy—

ALEX *looks at him:* Moses, you have to work with what there is to work with. You accept the people you have to accept and that doesn't mean you always like them or always trust them.

CASSIE: Sometimes that's a dangerous game, Alex. And it seems to me I've heard you say those words before. *Laughs.* I remember: you and Mr. Taney and Rome in 1922— *She breaks off suddenly and suddenly stops laughing. Emily rises quickly, moves to the bell cord, pulls it, stands quietly near the door.*

MOSES: A very dangerous game. Mr. Wilson played it. It goes on the assumption that bad men are stupid and good men are smart, and all diplomats are both good *and* smart. Well, the last time, Mr. Clemenceau was both very bad and very smart. Why don't you people ever read a book?

EMILY: Is it like old times, Cassie? Father and Alex—

CASSIE: Yes. It's as if I'd never been away from here.

EMILY *carefully:* You were saying it was like that day in Rome. That famous, famous day.

SAM: Famous for what?

ALEX *quickly:* Mussolini took over the city that day.

EMILY *looks at him, laughs:* Yes. *Ponette appears in the hall door.* Isn't dinner ready, Ponette? It's late.

PONETTE: It has been ready for a half hour.

EMILY: It was thought best not to tell me?

PONETTE: I think perhaps I did come to tell you. Or I think perhaps I did not.

ALEX: Well, I think perhaps we can dine. *Comes toward Cassie as if to take her in.* Cassie— *As he reaches her he stops, looks at her, turns away, goes quickly toward hall door. Sam has risen and is moving toward the hall door. Moses and Cassie also move toward it.*

MOSES *to Cassie, suddenly, as if he had just remembered:* Of course, my dear. I remember that day in Rome. That was the time I duennaed you and Emily to Italy. And you and I and Sophronia came home alone and Emily stayed on to play the piano. That was the day I decided to retire and let the world go to hell without my help.

Alex has stopped to listen. Then quickly moves on, passes through the door.

SAM *as he gets to the door, to Emily:* Were you and Father married then?

EMILY: No, darling. That was 1922. You weren't born until '24, and you're legitimate.

MOSES *as he takes Sam's arm:* Certainly are. Everything was quite in order. *They go to the door.*

CASSIE *smiles, nervously:* Why are we talking so much about the past? Are martinis for remembrance?

EMILY: It's natural to talk about it. We haven't seen each other for so long. It's natural we remember what used to be.

CASSIE *softly:* Is it natural? I have the feeling you wanted us to remember.

EMILY *after a second, shrugs, softly:* Let it come as it will, Cas. Better for all of us if we're not frightened of it.

CASSIE *turns:* Frightened of what? What do you mean, Em? *As if she wants to move toward the hall:* Why did you ask me here, why did I come? It's too difficult for us to meet again. Why did you ask me, why did I come?—

EMILY: Because we wanted to see each other again.

CASSIE *slowly:* I don't think that's the truth.

EMILY *pleasantly:* I don't think so either. Come along to dinner, Cas. *Cassie turns slowly toward the door. As she turns, she drops her evening bag. Both of them stare at it.* Remember the tennis match and how you broke your racket and then you dropped your mother's best cut-glass punch bowl? And at college, before exams, you always dropped everything? Whenever you were frightened or nervous you'd always drop things. *Before Cassie can move, Emily stoops down to pick up the bag.*

CASSIE *takes the bag, looks steadily at Emily:* That's right, Em. Everybody does something when they get nervous: you speak more slowly. You always did. *Smiles.* You're doing it now.

EMILY *speaks very slowly, as if on purpose:* I know. Come along now.

As they go through the door,

CURTAIN FALLS

Act One: Scene 2

The living room of a suite in the Grand Hotel, Rome, October 1922. The furniture has been pushed from the center of the room to allow space for three large trunks. The trunks are open and partly packed. A couch and two chairs have been arranged near the large, center windows. A piano is in one corner of the room. Downstage, left, there is a door leading to a bedroom; upstage, right, there is a door leading to another bedroom; downstage, right, is a door leading to the hotel corridor. Near the left bedroom door is a table on which is a news ticker. As the curtain rises, Sophronia, about forty years old, is in the upstage left corner, ironing underwear at a board. A few seconds after the curtain rises there is the sound of guns. Sophronia puts down her iron, goes to the window, opens it. As she opens the window, the gun sounds increase and then suddenly die away. The telephone rings.

SOPHRONIA *crosses to the phone, picks it up:* Hello. Hello. Hello. Oh. No, Mr. Hazen. Like I told you. He hasn't been asleep at all, but I don't think he'll come to the phone. The girls are up, but they haven't come in for breakfast. No, sir, if anybody's frightened they haven't showed it to me. All right, I'll— *Crosses to the bedroom door on left, knocks. There is no answer; she knocks again. Then she opens the door.* Mr. Taney, it's Alex Hazen on the phone again. *No answer.* He says the Ambassador told him to tell you, you and the girls and me should come and stay in the Embassy until our boat leaves. Mr. Hazen says he'll come down in an Embassy car and take us—

MOSES' VOICE: Tell Alex to tell the Ambassador to go to hell.

SOPHRONIA: You better tell him that yourself.

MOSES' VOICE: Shut the door, Sophronia.

SOPHRONIA *crosses to phone:* Mr. Taney says to thank the Ambassador, but we'll stay here. *Hangs up phone, goes back to ironing board. After a second there is a knock on the door that leads to the corridor. She looks up as the door opens and a table is wheeled in by an Elderly Waiter. He is followed by a Young Waiter, very thin, very stoop-shouldered. The Elderly Waiter wheels the table to the middle of the floor. The Young Waiter is carrying a large ovenish affair. The Elderly Waiter arranges chairs at the table, puts out the fruit, etc.*

ELDERLY WAITER, *as he speaks there is again the booming of faraway guns, and what he says is not clearly heard:* Il direttore dice di preghare tutti gli ospite di non spaventarsi. *The guns die off. Sophronia does not answer him. He turns to the Young Waiter:* Gli parlero io.

YOUNG WAITER *with the accent of an Italian who has learned to speak English in London. He is a tired man and he speaks like one:* He says the manager will call on all guests to tell them not to be frightened by guns. Nobody, he says, need be frightened in the city of Rome, Italy.

SOPHRONIA: Good.

*The Elderly Waiter looks at the Young Waiter. The Young
Waiter shrugs, nods. The Elderly Waiter says "Resti," exits.
There is a long pause.*

YOUNG WAITER *begins to cough. He tries hard to stifle it.
He coughs hard, as if it hurts him. He looks at Sophronia,
frightened. Then he backs up to the wall, as if to rest
against it. Sophronia crosses to the table, picks up a glass
of water, takes it to him. He hesitates, drinks, stops cough-
ing. Quickly:* I did not cough near the table. I—

SOPHRONIA *as he starts to cough again:* Sit down. *She pushes
a chair toward him. He sits down, looks up at her, smiles
warmly.*

YOUNG WAITER *after a moment:* You will not report I
cough near the table?

SOPHRONIA: What's the matter with you?"

YOUNG WAITER *quickly:* From the cigarettes. *Then shrugs.*
My lungs are bad from the war. This is my second day
here, in Grand Hotel, and if I am reported to be sick—

*Sophronia has moved away from him toward the oven.
She takes out a large thermos of coffee, opens the top,
smells it, pours coffee into a cup.*

SOPHRONIA *brings him the cup:* Have it. Good for your
cough.

YOUNG WAITER *hesitates, then takes it eagerly:* You are
kind.

*The left bedroom door opens and Moses, in a dressing
gown, comes in. Moses is about fifty years old.*

YOUNG WAITER *jumps to his feet, holds out the cup to Sophronia, backs away from the door:* I—your pardon. I—

MOSES *goes to the ticker-tape, picks it up:* What's the matter?

SOPHRONIA *turns to the table to pour coffee for Moses:* He coughs because he got hurt in the war, and now he's scared to death you're going to get mad because he drinks a cup of coffee. They're all scared. I'm sick of it. Everybody's got the same look. You come to Europe next summer, you come without me.

MOSES *wearily:* All right. All right. We're going home. *Sophronia goes toward Moses' room; exits.* Sit down, Waiter, and finish your coffee.

The guns begin again. The noise is still far away, but there are more guns now and steadier firing.

MOSES *reads from the ticker-tape. Laughs unpleasantly:* The government is in control. King Victor Emmanuel returned this morning from bathing in the sea. The stories of Mussolini's armies are lies. He is not marching on the city. But everybody is to stay off the streets in case he is— *Throws down the tape.* Those are the government guns. They are not being answered. A child of six would conclude they are not being fired at anything, and won't be. The bastards are putting on a fake show and they won't even spend the money for a good one. *Laughs.* Well, that means Signor Mussolini should be in the city in a few hours.

YOUNG WAITER *takes dishes out of oven, brings them to Moses. Speaks cautiously:* I am told many foreigners here think it wise, sir.

MOSES: Yes, many foreigners. Are you a Fascist?

YOUNG WAITER: No, sir. I am not.

MOSES: You must feel out of place. Everybody else in the hotel is.

YOUNG WAITER *smiles:* In every hotel. They live to please those who give orders.

MOSES: How many men do you think Mussolini's got? I've heard everything from sixty thousand to six hundred.

YOUNG WAITER: Not sixty thousand. My brother-in-law is one of them. He laughs and says the government garrison could stop them, but the garrison will not. He says the King and the Government are with the Fascisti now and want them to march in. What do you think, sir?

MOSES: Your brother-in-law is right. It's all finished now.

YOUNG WAITER: It has been finished for a long time.

MOSES: When was it finished for you?

YOUNG WAITER: It does not finish like a clock, or begin like one, either.

MOSES *slowly:* No, but I guess all of us want to know when things happened. Or when we first should have realized they were happening. I've been awake all night. *Motions toward the window.* Not with this. I knew most of this a year ago. But I should have known before that, and I did. But I didn't know I did. All night I've been trying to find out when I should have known.

YOUNG WAITER *softly:* For me, for many Italians, it was there in 1919, three years ago. Your President Wilson came to speak to us, in the Piazza Venezia. It meant much to us. The great man would speak to us, tell us what to do, tell us how to make a free country. Fifty thousand people came. Many of them walked all night. They carried their children— *Looks at Moses, turns away.* I speak too much. *Moses shakes his head.* But our King and our Government did not wish President Wilson to speak. They were afraid of us. All day they keep him inside the palace, meeting the great names who came to call. All day the people waited, until night time. Night time it was too late. I waited with the last. I did not know it then, but that night it was finished for me.

MOSES *gets up:* Wilson is a man who likes fancy words and fancy names. That's one of the things I didn't know in time. I am sorry for that. I might have saved you some of this. *Moses goes to the window. There is a long silence.*

YOUNG WAITER *speaks timidly:* Shall I wait to serve, sir?

MOSES *without turning:* No, thank you. Good luck, some day.

YOUNG WAITER *as he exits:* Thank you, sir. To you, also.

The guns begin again. They are loud now and over them are the muffled sounds of distant shouting. The noises are sharp, mixed, and frightening. The left bedroom door opens and Emily, in a dressing gown, comes quickly in. She is twenty-two years old. She crosses to the window.

EMILY: Is it going to be bad, Father?

MOSES: It has been bad, it is bad, and it is going to be bad. *As he speaks, Cassie comes in. She is twenty-two years old. She has on a dressing gown. The noise of the guns begins to die away.*

EMILY: It seems to me all we've ever known, since we grew up, are wars and revolutions.

MOSES: I'll tell them to stop it. I'll say that revolutions disturb you.

CASSIE *laughs, pours herself a cup of coffee, takes it to the window:* They weren't very disturbed at Mrs. Hayworth's last night. Mrs. Hayworth has met Mussolini. She admires him. So did everybody there.

EMILY: Did you see Ann Hayworth and Jamie? Reeling around drunk and their mother didn't even seem to notice. We looked like flowers from a Victorian garden. Flowers. Send flowers, Father, with apologies.

MOSES *glares at her:* Did the guns interfere with Mrs. Hayworth's chamber music?

EMILY: No. Nobody seemed nervous. Signor Orlando was very disappointed you didn't come to dinner. He said he hadn't seen you since the Peace Conference but that he always read your articles. He said you were a great liberal, a great man.

MOSES: Did you tell him I thought he was a son of a bitch?

EMILY *laughs:* I would have, Father, if you had told me in time. You were generally admired. A man called Perrone said he'd only come because he thought you might be there. He said he didn't think you understood the situation here and he wanted to talk to you about it. He hoped Mussolini would take over the government. He said the Fascisti will mean a recovery for Italy—

MOSES: He's an impartial judge. He put up the money for Mussolini.

EMILY *smiles:* He didn't mention that. He said the Fascist leaders were true idealists—

CASSIE: And would return to Rome the glory of Caesar—

MOSES: Is one allowed to spit at Mrs. Hayworth's table?

EMILY *laughs:* You always told me not to spit at dinner.

MOSES: I've changed my mind.

EMILY: Then it's just as well you weren't there. Alex didn't come, either, and Cassie came home early with a headache. I'll send flowers for you.

MOSES *sharply:* You will not send flowers, you will not make an apology, and you will not go to the Hayworths' again.

He moves to his room as Sophronia comes from his room. She is carrying clothes. He goes into the room, closes the door. Sophronia puts the clothes on top of Moses' trunk, crosses to the right bedroom door.

SOPHRONIA: Did your laundry come back?

Emily has picked up the morning mail and is opening it. Cassie has taken a letter from the pile and is reading it.

EMILY: No, ma'am.

SOPHRONIA: I told you to phone for it. *She goes into the bedroom.*

EMILY: Now *there's* a good-humored pair to have on a vacation. I wish we could go back to Paris for a few weeks. I think I'll ask Father— *Reading from the letter:* Sarah Sturgis is getting married. Well. She says she hopes we're home for the wedding.

CASSIE *looks up from her letter:* Dr. Pierce says it's all right. The board of trustees has approved me. I can come back to college and teach. English department at fifteen hundred a year.

EMILY *looks up:* I didn't know you had been writing to Pierce. I thought you were coming back to Washington and stay with us for a while until you decided what you really wanted to do.

CASSIE: Father can't afford anything any more. I've got to have a job right away.

EMILY: Oh, what difference does the money make? *Points to Moses' door.* Father's got plenty and in a few months I'll have all that Mother left me. Who wants to teach? Certainly not you. Come back and stay with us until you find something that's fun—

CASSIE: Thanks, Em. Really thanks. But I'm going to cable him today I'll take the job. It won't be bad—for a while, anyway.

EMILY *looks at Cassie:* I don't understand why you didn't tell me.

CASSIE: I've known for a long time it would have to be. There was no need of talking about it until I had the job. *Quickly:* What else does Sarah say?

EMILY *looks at Cassie, then goes back to the letter, laughs:* Oh. She says she told George that she'd had a beau before him, and he didn't seem to mind much, and she says that settles all the arguments— My entire memory of college is a discussion of whether you ought to have an affair before you marry and if you do, should you tell your husband? *Laughs.* Baby talk. None of us would ever have had the nerve—except Sarah and then she had to get so drunk she couldn't remember a single interesting detail to tell us. Remember how daring we thought her?

CASSIE: I don't think even then I thought it daring. There's nothing daring about it.

EMILY *smiles:* How do you know, Cas?

CASSIE *arranging the drawers of her trunk. She hesitates and then speaks quickly:* I did have a headache last night. But that isn't why I left the Hayworths'. I met Alex.

EMILY *after a second:* You mean you met him in the lobby downstairs or—

CASSIE: No. We had planned to meet.

EMILY *slowly:* How strange. Why should you and Alex *plan* to meet?

CASSIE: Why not?

EMILY: What do you mean "why not"? We've grown up with Alex Hazen. We always saw him together. What— *She gets up.* I understand. So it's not very daring. *Very slowly:* We've known each other all our lives. But sometimes I don't think we understand each other, Cas. I never thought you and Alex got along very well. You're so unlike. *Quickly:* And then, of course, I suppose I'd always thought I might marry him some day—

CASSIE *quickly, sharply:* I didn't know that. And I know he doesn't know it. You made it up this minute—

EMILY: I didn't say he knew it. I said that sometimes I thought that—

CASSIE *slowly:* Then it was a fantasy, Emily. And as dangerous as most.

EMILY: Yes. What plans have you got? The two of you, I mean.

CASSIE: None. I—

EMILY *comes to her:* Cassie, talk to me. Tell me things. Because otherwise we might get mixed up, or—

CASSIE *carefully:* We have nothing you would call plans. I suppose we said all the things people have always said to each other. *Suddenly points to the window.* It's not a good time to talk about oneself. So much important happening to so many people—

EMILY: What high-falutin' talk, Cas. You sound like Father, only he means it. You know that no matter what happens any place in the world, people go on talking about themselves, and always say they haven't because they think it sounds better that way. *She turns, exits. Cassie stands looking after her as Sophronia comes into the room.*

SOPHRONIA *calling back to Emily:* Put the stuff that's for the trunks on the bed and the stuff that's for the valises— *As Sophronia crosses toward the corridor door, a dressy, excited man opens the door. He looks like any manager of any fancy hotel.*

MANAGER: Signori, Messieurs, Mesdames. Do not be uneasy. I have full assurance that the Grand Hotel will be protected. Please do not leave your beautiful apartments. All will be taken care of—

Alexander Hazen, twenty-seven years old, tries to push past him.

MANAGER *turns to Alex:* Monsieur, no strangers are allowed in the hotel. You must not fly through the halls frightening the guests— *Alex pushes him aside. Sophronia comes to the door. Manager speaks to her:* You cannot leave the apartment. My orders—

SOPHRONIA *shoves him:* I need the laundry. Move.

ALEX *to Manager:* I'm Hazen from the American Embassy. Close the door, please.

MANAGER: Oh. Then. The people from the newspapers downstairs, could you not take them away—

ALEX *as the Manager closes the door:* It took me an hour to come six blocks. It's hell outside. Italians are excitable people.

CASSIE: I guess we'd be, too, if that was happening outside.

ALEX: The Ambassador wants all of you brought to the Embassy right away. We have assurances that no American will be touched, but with that crew outside, you can't tell. What's the matter?

CASSIE: Nothing.

ALEX: Where's Mr. Taney?

CASSIE: He won't go to the Embassy, and you know it.

ALEX: All right. But I want to talk to him about something else: the A.P., Reuters, Havas are downstairs. I want to ask him—

CASSIE *points toward window:* What will happen?

ALEX: Second secretaries aren't told much. But I think

they've decided to let Mussolini in. The government soldiers are really there to see that nobody stops him.

CASSIE *sharply:* It's a dirty, dirty mess. What is the Ambassador going to do about it?

ALEX: Cassie, you asked me the same thing last night. What can he do? He's here to represent the United States and not to fight in civil wars. I can't seem to make you understand—

CASSIE: Perhaps because you don't really understand it yourself.

ALEX: I don't think I do. But I know you don't, darling.

CASSIE: We're an ignorant generation. We see so much and know so little. Maybe because we think about ourselves so much. I just told Emily that, and she said I was faking. *Turns to him:* She said that you and I never got along very well— *As if to herself:* We don't really agree. And most of the time we don't know what we're disagreeing about.

ALEX: That's right. That's because you've decided I'm on something you call the other side. Although I don't think you know what you mean by that.

CASSIE: A revolution is going on outside. But by this time next year it will be nothing more than dinner-table conversation. Things mean so little to us—

ALEX: They mean a lot to me. I've been trying hard to figure them out. People like me didn't have much time to think. A few years of college, then the army—

CASSIE: And now three years of the Embassy. More than you know, you've come to think the way they think—

ALEX: For God's sake, Cassie, if you disapprove of me so much, why did you sleep with me? I don't believe people in love fight about things like this. They only use it as an excuse. It must be something else— *Puts his arms around her.* Are you in love with me?

CASSIE *softly:* I don't know. I think so. Are you, with me?

ALEX: Yes. Very much. Cassie, stay here. Stay in Rome with me. We'll find out here—

CASSIE *very quickly, very nervously:* No, no. I can't. I want to go home and think about us. I couldn't stay here and see these people and lead this life and still think straight. I'm mixed up about everything. I want to be alone and find out what I feel, what I want, what I want for you and me.

ALEX: All right, darling. I'll be coming back to Washington for Christmas. I know what I want. By then I want to know what you want.

CASSIE: Yes. Yes. In a few months maybe I'll make sense— *Grips his arm.* I told Emily about us. And she was upset. She said— *Tensely:* What's the difference what she said? This is a bad day. The guns outside seem to have come in here, and I don't want to think—

ALEX *puzzled:* All right, darling, all right. *As he leans down to kiss her, Moses comes in from the bedroom.*

MOSES: There must have been people who kissed through the French Revolution. I am in a bad humor; go down in the lobby and make love.

ALEX: We can't. It's filled with excited international ladies and gentlemen asking excited international questions.

Also, the newspaper people waiting to see you— *His last words are drowned out by loud shouting. Then there are three gun shots. As Cassie moves to the window, he shouts at her:* Get away from the window, Cas. *He puts his hand to his face.* I wish they'd get this over with. One way or—

MOSES *as the shouting dies down:* They will. Like an operation. Just a few minutes more, and the patient will be an invalid for life. How's the Ambassador taking all this?

ALEX: Do you mean is Ambassador Child upset about his wife and children? Or—

MOSES: That is not what I meant. You are learning well. All diplomacy starts with learning to ask a question if you don't want to answer one.

ALEX: I can't speak for the Ambassador.

The door flies open and the Hotel Manager is propelled into the room. Behind him are two Fascist Soldiers.

MANAGER: Please control your fears. All is under control in the hotel. Please do not shout and cry out—

ALEX *angrily:* You were here with that once before.

MANAGER: These two soldiers of Signor Mussolini are present only to certify the guests— Signor Taney, Signorina Bowman— *The ticker-tape begins to click.*

MOSES: Shut up. *Goes to the machine, reads from the tape:* A proclamation has been given to the press. King Victor Emmanuel has asked Benito Mussolini to form a government. Proclamation to the people of Rome by the King of Italy reads: "My people, I wish to ask you—"*Moses throws down the tape, looks at the two Soldiers. At the same minute, Emily opens her bedroom door.*

MANAGER *nervously, to Soldiers:* Sono degli Americani. Sono dei signori molto distinti.

MOSES *slowly, softly:* Get yourself and these swine out of here.

MANAGER *shrilly:* Signor, I must ask you—

SOLDIER: Casa dice?

MANAGER *to Soldiers:* Dice lui—dice lui che partiránno stasera.

MOSES: I said no such thing. *To Soldiers:* I said Volevo voi altri porci via di quà.

The First Soldier moves quickly toward Moses. Alex moves up to the Soldier, pushes him back. The Second Soldier moves forward.

SOLDIER: Vecchio diavlo!

ALEX *quickly:* American Embassy. There will be no trouble. L'ambasciata Americana. Non a sera nessun disturbo. Per piacere, andate via.

FIRST SOLDIER: Va bene. Andiamo.

The Soldier hesitates, then turns, motions to the Manager and to the Second Soldier. They go out and the Second Soldier slams the door. The Manager, shocked at the slamming, opens the door, looks in, smiles, says "Mi scusi," softly closes the door. Emily laughs.

EMILY: What was all that?

ALEX: That was your father. *Crosses to Moses.* I came through the war without getting killed. Therefore, I don't intend to get shot in a hotel room because you are a brave man.

MOSES *laughs, unpleasantly:* I agree with you. I will not show off again.

EMILY *to Cassie:* Your stuff is ready to be packed now, Cassie.

ALEX *sharply:* Mr. Taney, we heard that you were about to give out a statement. The newspaper people are waiting downstairs. You are a powerful man at home and your paper is a powerful paper. Any statement you give will be dangerous to the relations between our country and Italy. The Ambassador feels that we cannot take sides in an internal uprising—

MOSES *sharply:* Stop that foolish talk. He long ago took sides. And so, I think, did you.

ALEX *comes to Moses, softly:* You've been ragging me for years, Mr. Taney. I don't usually mind it. I do today. *Points to the window.* I can only speak for myself. I don't like this, and I don't like your thinking I do. But another few months of the kind of misery and starvation they've had, and there would have been a revolution. If Mussolini can put it down that doesn't make me like him, or the money behind him, or the people. But somebody had to do it, and you don't pick gentlemen to do the job. You were at the Peace Conference and you know that wasn't wild talk about Communism in Italy. *Slowly, carefully:* And now I am going to tell you, Mr. Taney, that with all your liberal beliefs, I do not believe you wanted that. *There is a pause, and he moves away.*

MOSES: That's well said, and mostly true. *Sharply:* But I didn't want this and I have fought hard, in my way, to stop it. I like people, and I don't like to see them put down by gangsters who make a job of doing it for those who want it done. *Very sharply:* Don't worry, and tell your boss not to worry. I'll give no interviews and write no pieces. I want no more of any of it. Anywhere. I'm through with the paper. *Slowly, wearily, he goes toward his room.* I want to cry. And you should want to cry. You are young. This is a sad day, and you will pay for it. Whenever such things happen, the rest of the world some day pays for them. It's going to be over for me now, but it's just beginning for you. *He goes into room.*

EMILY *after a minute:* Well.

ALEX *uncomfortably:* He's making too much of it all. They're only exchanging one bad lot for another. But I admire your father, even when I don't agree with him or know what he's talking about. Ach. Nobody knows what they're talking about. Least of all me. *Moves toward corridor door.* I'll see you later.

CASSIE *goes toward bedroom door:* All right. *Goes into her room, does not close the door.*

ALEX: I'll be back in time to take you to the station.

EMILY *slowly:* I've been thinking. I don't think I'll go. I want to go on with my music lessons. I've enjoyed them here— I don't want to go home yet. I think I'll stay here for a few months and—

ALEX: It's no time to be staying here. You can't stay alone, and Cassie wants to get back— Anyway, your father wouldn't like it—

EMILY *smiles:* You forget that I don't have to ask any more. I'm a great heiress. Anyway, he won't care. *Gaily:* You could beau me around. We've known each other so long that there wouldn't be any gossip—

ALEX: I've got to get back. See you later. I think you better change your mind— *Exits.*

Emily stands looking after him. Then she begins to move about the room, idly, as if she were thinking. She goes to the piano, sits down, begins to play. As she plays, the guns start again, louder and closer than before. Cassie appears in the bedroom door carrying underwear and a box: She stands in the doorway looking at Emily.

EMILY: Why don't you stay in Rome, Cassie? Why are you leaving Alex now?

CASSIE: Do stop playing the piano. It doesn't go well with guns.

EMILY: Nothing goes well with guns. You haven't answered me. And yet it might be wise to be honest with me about what you feel—

CASSIE *quickly:* I've been honest with you.

EMILY *after a second:* I guess you don't want to talk to me. Now that I think back there were so many times, even when we were little girls, when that was true. Maybe it's best that you and I should be away from each other for a while. I've decided not to sail with you and Father. I'm going to stay here. I'll ask Aunt Sophie to come. We'll take a house, I think, for a few months— *Cassie drops the box that she is holding. Emily peers over the piano, sees that*

Cassie is staring at her. What's the matter, Cassie? Why are you dropping things? That means you're nervous or hiding something. What is there to be nervous about or to hide?

As Cassie leans down to pick up the box,

CURTAIN FALLS

Act One: Scene 3

The drawing room of the Hazen house, about nine-thirty the same evening as Scene I.
As the curtain rises Sophronia is moving about the room emptying ash trays. On the center table is a silver tray with coffee, liqueurs, a brandy decanter, cups, etc. Ponette is sitting next to the table, watching Sophronia.

PONETTE *twists to look at the hall door, sighs, adjusts the cups on the tray:* Long dinner.

SOPHRONIA: Try to stay awake for a few minutes longer.

PONETTE: Two Chablis and two Haut Brion for five people is most extravagant. *Leans forward, intimately:* I did not like the conversation at dinner. Much of it I did not understand, but much of it I did not like. For four bottles of wine people should be lighter, with jokes. Did you?

SOPHRONIA *irritably:* Did I what?

PONETTE: The talk, the attitude, the tone.

SOPHRONIA *very sharply:* I wasn't listening.

PONETTE *giggles:* That is not true. Mr. Taney asked you if it was not the 28th of October, that day in Rome, and you say no, it was the 29th. You could not answer if you did not listen. *After a pause, bored:* Corporal Hazen does not eat much dinner. He looks bad today, sick.

SOPHRONIA *angrily:* What are you talking about? Sam wasn't hungry tonight. I'll make something for him later. He doesn't look sick at all.

PONETTE: He does not act well. John told me.

SOPHRONIA: Sam's getting along fine. Is John a doctor now?

PONETTE: John drive him today to the hospital. Corporal Hazen go in. A little time go by, the Corporal comes out, looks bad in the face, gets in the car, sits there. Ten, twenty minutes, maybe, John says he sits there, says nothing. Finally, John turns around and the Corporal says, "John, don't tell anybody we came to the hospital." *Shrugs.* I am nobody, perhaps, so John tell me—

SOPHRONIA *quickly, tensely:* Go out to the garage and tell John I want to see him in the kitchen right away.

PONETTE *shakes his head:* Mrs. Hazen tells John she does not need car, so he goes to the movies. If it were me, I walk. The night is lovely, the moon is high.

SOPHRONIA: All right, poet. Take the coffee back to your wife and see if she can reheat it without blowing up the stove.

PONETTE: It still steams.

SOPHRONIA: Take it back.

He sighs, rises, picks up the tray, starts for the hall door. As he reaches it, Emily and Cassie come slowly in.

PONETTE *bows to Emily, points to tray:* I will return, Madame Hazen.

Emily stares at him as if she were thinking of something else. As Sophronia speaks, Emily and Cassie move to the couch, sit down.

SOPHRONIA *to Ponette, as he exits:* Lucky, we are. *There is a pause as she moves about. She turns to look at Emily and Cassie, frowns, puzzled. After a second:* Nice to see you back, Miss Cassie.

CASSIE *looks up, as if she'd been thinking of something else:* Oh. Thank you, Sophronia. It's been good to see you again.

SOPHRONIA: How do you like Sam?

CASSIE: I like him. I can tell that you do, too.

SOPHRONIA *as if she wanted to be reassured, to Emily:* He looks better, doesn't he, Miss Emily? Don't you think he does?

EMILY *softly:* Yes, I think he does.

For a second Sophronia stands staring at them, then she goes out the dining hall door.

CASSIE *after a second, looks at Emily, awkwardly:* I have a headache. Too much talk about the past, I guess. Or maybe too much wine. I'm not used to drinking.

EMILY: None of us. I've always wondered if people drink because they want to talk or talk because they want to drink. Shall I get you something for your headache?

CASSIE: No, no. Thank you, Em. I can't stay late. I must be going soon—

Moses, Alex, and Sam come in from the dining hall door.

They, too, come in slowly, as if they were thinking. All three turn to look at Cassie and Emily.

MOSES *too brightly:* We decided to have our coffee in here with you. Filthy habit, leaving the men at the table. Arrange to stop it, Emily.

EMILY: I didn't start it, Father. You've been doing it ever since I can remember.

MOSES *sits down:* That's true enough. I used to want it because two hours of your mother at dinner were long enough. Emily, you're old enough for me to tell you that I didn't like your mother.

EMILY *quietly:* I always knew it, Father. Children don't miss things like that.

MOSES: I felt sorry when she died, but all I remember now is that I said, to *myself,* of course, "Really, my dear, you didn't have to go that far to accommodate me." It's a bad thing not to love the woman you live with. It tells on a man.

CASSIE: Tells on a woman, too, I should think.

MOSES *nods:* Comes out in ways you don't recognize. Now you take your father, Alex. Same thing with him. He didn't like your stepmother. So what did he do? He fell in love with the State Department and that's nothing to climb into bed with on a wintry night.

EMILY *looks at Sam:* Stop frowning, Sam. It's bad for the young.

SAM: I was thinking that you often know more about people in books than—than I've known about any of you,

I guess. *To Alex:* I didn't know you had been in Italy
when Fascism first started. There you were on such a big
day and it was so important how you figured out that day.
Or maybe I only think so because I was there and saw
what it did— *Lamely:* I can't seem to say what I mean.

ALEX: You mean that if people like me had seen it straight,
maybe you wouldn't have had to be there twenty-two years
later.

EMILY *softly:* But most people don't see things straight on
the day they happen. It takes years to understand—

SAM: If that were true then everybody would understand
everything too late.

ALEX: There are men who see their own time as clearly as
if it were history. But they're very rare, Sam. *To Moses:*
And before you speak, I want to say I don't think you're
one of them.

MOSES *laughs:* I don't think so either. *Gaily:* Just because
I understood things quicker than you did, didn't make
me smart, if you know what I mean.

ALEX: I do.

SAM *as if to himself:* I'd like to learn how to put things together, see them when they come—

EMILY: Maybe you will, darling. *Sophronia reappears with
the coffee tray, brandy, glasses.* It's what everybody wants
to do. Don't let us discourage you. Our generation made
quite a mess. Come and have coffee on the terrace. Father,
Sam. It's a lovely night.

MOSES: I don't like the terrace. I hate those damn chairs.

EMILY *turns to look at him:* Come, Father, please.

MOSES *sighs, moves toward the terrace:* What's the matter with you tonight?

As Sam begins to move toward the terrace, Sophronia comes to him.

SOPHRONIA: You should go back to bed, Sam. You've been up too long. *She is now very close to him. She speaks softly.* Why did you go to the hospital?

SAM *puts his arm around her, very quickly:* If you don't stop fussing about me I may shoot you. *He looks down at her, shakes his head. She stares at him, nods. He puts his face against her hair, presses her arm, and moves to the terrace. Sophronia exits through the hall door. Emily comes out to the terrace.*

MOSES *squirming around in the chair:* You all right, Sam? Damn chairs. Why would anybody make furniture out of wicker and then try to pad it with these things that move around? Emily, I'm getting too old—

EMILY *laughs:* I'll buy you a box of that candy you like, Father, if you'll shut up for just five minutes. *She puts her hand on Sam's arm, smiles at him.*

Cassie crosses to Alex, who is standing near the piano.

ALEX *softly:* Why did you come tonight, Cassie? And why didn't you tell me? *As she looks nervously toward the terrace:* Don't worry. Emily has arranged this for us.

CASSIE *softly:* Remember? A long time ago, I asked you if you were going to feel guilty. I told you then I didn't want it that way—

ALEX: And I told you then that it was between me and you, and me and Emily. I don't feel guilty, and you haven't answered me.

CASSIE *nervously:* Emily called me at the Taylors'. Twice. I didn't know what to say—

ALEX *frowns:* Simple to say you couldn't come, or didn't want to. What's the sense of sitting at a dinner table and talking about twenty-two years ago—

CASSIE *sharply:* I didn't start that talk, Alex. And I didn't say anything that all of us didn't know.

ALEX *looks around the room, nervously:* I don't understand what this is all about. I— Why did you tell Emily we had dinner together last night, when you meant last week?

CASSIE *tensely:* I don't know. It was a slip. I didn't mean to say it. I don't like tonight any better than you do, and I don't like the way you're talking to me.

ALEX *touches her hand:* I'm sorry, Cas. I—

EMILY *comes in from the terrace:* It's warm and pleasant. Won't you come on the terrace, Cassie?

CASSIE *gets up:* I must go now, Em.

EMILY: Why?

CASSIE: Why? Because it's late. *Looks at Emily, softly:* And because I think it was wrong for us to meet again, and because it's never a good idea to talk about the past. Let's remember by ourselves, Em, with the lights out. *She moves toward the door. Emily moves with her.*

EMILY: No. *In front of Cassie.* No.

CASSIE *after a second, quietly:* I want to go, Em.

EMILY: No.

ALEX *comes to Emily:* What is it? What's?—

EMILY: I don't want Cassie to leave. This has been coming for a good many years. We've started it; let's finish it.

ALEX *after a second, softly:* Whatever you want to know, Em, I'll tell you. It's between you and me, and we can do it alone.

EMILY *softly:* I know what you would tell me. I've known for a long time. But there's a great deal that you don't know, and Cassie doesn't know, and I don't, either. It's time to find out.

Alex looks at her. Then, after a pause, he moves quickly to the terrace doors. As he moves, Sam gets up, stands in the door. As Alex reaches the doors and moves as if to close them, Sam puts his cane against the door.

SAM: If you and Mother would let me, I'd rather stay. I don't know what's happening, but I have a feeling it's got to do with me, too. Anyway, it's kind of an important night for me because—well, just because.

EMILY *after a second:* You can stay, Sam.

CASSIE *tensely, turns to Emily:* Leave it alone, Em. Leave it alone. It's no good for people to sit in a room and talk about what they were, or what they wanted, or what they might have been—

EMILY *softly:* Yes, it's hard. For all of us. It scares me, too.

ALEX *comes to her:* What is it you want? What are you doing?

EMILY *simply:* I don't know, Alex. But maybe we'll find out. *Pleasantly:* Sit down, Cassie. Please.

CURTAIN FALLS

Act Two: Scene 1

The corner of a restaurant in Berlin, the autumn of 1923.
One table faces the audience and several other tables, in an
off-stage alcove, can be seen. Back of the table is a large
window, partly opened, hung with heavy draperies.
Alex is sitting at the table, a cocktail in front of him. He
is looking at a menu card. Standing next to the table is
Eppler, a middle-aged German who owns the restaurant.
He is holding a pad, waiting to take Alex's order.

EPPLER *after a second:* The Rostbraten, maybe? Mrs.
Hazen liked it so much the last week we had it. Notice the
price mounts. This morning I buy bread for one hundred
and forty billion marks the loaf. You are lucky to have
American money.

ALEX: I'm ashamed to use it with things as they are.

EPPLER *laughs, looks around the restaurant:* There are not
many such who are ashamed. In all my years in business I
have not seen so many American dollars and English
pounds. Here now they buy a drink for more than a German can earn in a week. It is the fault of no one, but it
causes bad feeling. You understand, Mr. Hazen. It is not
wise to have rich tourists here now. You work in Berlin,
you understand that.

ALEX: I understand, of course. But we can't keep them home. And your government seems to want them here.

EPPLER *wearily:* Ach, I know. It goes in a circle. I no longer know what it is. Bread for a hundred and forty billion marks. It is crazy— *Through his speech there is the noise of a distant commotion. Now the noise comes nearer; it is the noise of a large mob, four or five blocks away, shouting and running. The words of the shouting are confused, but through them, at intervals, come "Juden. Judenstrasse. Juden." The Guests in the restaurant rush to the aisles; the Waiters pause and then move toward Eppler. Alex rises. Eppler moves toward the doors as five or six men come running past the window.*

EPPLER *yells above the noise:* Die Türen zu. Die Türen zu.

ONE OF THE MEN *in the street pauses, looks in the window, laughs, calls in:* Wir gehen auf die Juden los. Heraus mit denen die hier sind.

WAITER *who is near Alex's table, shouting:* Schwein, Schwein.

ALEX *grabs the Waiter:* Did I understand what he said? Did I?—

WAITER: He said they are going after the Jews. He said if we had any here we should bring them out. *The Waiter moves hurriedly toward the windows, closes them, draws the curtains. There has been the noise of slamming doors, People talking loudly and excitedly, Eppler screaming instructions. Now Eppler comes down the aisle toward Alex's table.*

EPPLER *shouting to be heard:* Meine Herren, bleiben Sie sitzen. Die Polizei versichert alles unter Kontroll zu haben. Und auserden, die Unordnungen sind nicht in diese Gegend. Bitte, bleiben Sie sitzen.

UNSEEN MAN: What was it? What was it?

EPPLER *shouting over other voices:* The Freikorps, the Fascists, a bread riot and they went to the Jewish section—

VOICE *with an American accent:* What the hell is happening? Damn shame in the best restaurant in town—

EPPLER *screaming, nervous:* Please. Be seated. The doors have been closed. We cannot open them until the police tell us—

VOICE: We insist upon getting out of here. Open the doors—

EPPLER *to Alex:* Please, Mr. Hazen. Please say in English—

ALEX *turns to the restaurant:* I am Hazen of the American Embassy. Herr Eppler wishes me to tell you that there has been a disgraceful riot of hoodlums against the Jewish section. The police tell him that it is under control. In any case, it is not near here, but the doors must be kept closed until he is allowed to open them. Mr. Eppler asks you to go on with your lunch. There is nothing to be done now except by the police.

MAN: Disgraceful business. Yesterday—

WOMAN: How do we know they won't break in here? Why don't you get the police in here?—

EPPLER: Be calm. There is no danger here—

ALEX *to Eppler:* Please see that the door is opened for Mrs. Hazen when she comes.

EPPLER: Ladies and gentlemen, I am most sorry. *People who have been standing near Alex's table, move away. As they move away, Cassie is seen near the table, watching Alex.* Nothing such has happened here. I am most ashamed. Please resume your seats. *He moves off. Cassie comes closer to the table.*

CASSIE *softly:* Hard to believe that we would live to see a pogrom in the year 1923.

ALEX *as he looks up:* Yes. Very hard—

CASSIE *as he recognizes her:* It scares me, Alex. It scares me.

ALEX *gets up:* Cassie.

CASSIE: Hello, Alex.

ALEX *nervous, bewildered:* You here in Berlin?

CASSIE *smiles:* I seem to be.

ALEX: But you didn't phone us— Do sit down. Emily will be here any minute. Waiter, waiter. What will you drink, Cas? Will you have lunch with us? Are you with people?—

CASSIE *quietly:* Easy, easy. You're nervous about seeing me.

ALEX: It's a surprise, that's all. I don't— What will you have to drink, Cas, what?—

CASSIE *softly:* Do be quiet, Alex. For just a minute.

ALEX *nods, lowers his head. More steadily, after a minute:* When did you come over?

CASSIE: I've been in Paris for a month. I've been here for about a week. You've been here for seven months. You were changed from Rome, soon after the wedding. I know all about you.

ALEX *nervously:* But you didn't call us when you got here—

CASSIE *gently, touches his hand:* Look, Alex. You and I had a fight. It did bad things to me.

ALEX *slowly:* It did bad things to me too.

CASSIE: I know. And I wanted to wait until I could see you, well, without feeling—

ALEX *quickly:* Yes, I understand.

CASSIE: It's good to see you, Alex. I'd rather have had it some place else, on a calmer day, without all that outside— I should be very unhappy here. Don't you mind?

ALEX: It's a horrible place to be. But my job is here. I don't think I ever could have believed in such misery and poverty. They're desperate people.

CASSIE *who has been staring at him:* Are you— Are you glad to see me?

ALEX *looks up:* I don't know, Cas.

CASSIE: Has it been a good marriage?

ALEX *quickly:* Yes, it's been very good. And should you ask me questions like that? And should I be answering them?

CASSIE: Whose rules are those? I want to know about you.

ALEX: I want to know about you, too. *Simply, warmly:* I do like seeing you, Cas.

CASSIE: And I like seeing you. We've been so close to each other for so many years. It's made me sad to do without you, not to know about you—

Emily, followed by a Young Man, comes swiftly up to the table. Emily immediately sits down, begins to speak. The Young Man stands waiting.

EMILY: Alex, Alex. The car had to cross the Judenstrasse. They were dragging a man through the streets. And they were beating an old lady on the head. We got out and tried to get through to help them, and the crowd began to scream at us and push us back. They screamed after us that we were dirty Americans and to mind our business—

ALEX *to the Young Man:* What is it, Halsey? Somebody's leading it— It isn't coming from nowhere—

EMILY *softly:* Hello, Cas.

CASSIE: Hello, Emily.

HALSEY: The Freikorps people are in on it. Today's leaders were well dressed. I think its real leaders came from the Young People's League, just as they did last week. There's no question now it's tied up with the Bavarian trouble. The story around is that somebody from Thyssen put up the money for Ludendorff and for those clowns outside.

ALEX: That's hard to believe. He's a bad guy, but nobody's bad enough to put up the money for this—

CASSIE *laughs:* Dear Alex. You haven't changed. Nobody's that bad, even when the proof is outside the door.

ALEX: I didn't say the proof wasn't outside the door. I said I didn't believe a man like Thyssen—

EMILY *smiles:* It's like old times. You and Cassie.

ALEX *suddenly turns, stares at Emily and Cassie:* Emily, you weren't surprised that Cassie was here, you didn't seem—

EMILY: I forgot to be. It seemed so natural that the three of us should be together.

CASSIE: I don't think Emily and I could be surprised at seeing each other.

EMILY: No. And, of course, I did see you in here the other day. And you saw me.

ALEX: You saw each other the other day but you didn't speak?

HALSEY: Mr. Hazen, I've got the car outside. I'd better get back.

ALEX: I want to go to the police. We'll make a strong official protest. Put it on the grounds that many Americans are in Berlin—

CASSIE: The Embassy couldn't put it on the grounds that it's a horror and a disgrace. That would be too simple, wouldn't it?

ALEX *smiles:* Have dinner with us tonight and I'll tell you about it. *Leans down to kiss Emily.* Both of you stay here until I send Halsey back with the car. *As Alex kisses Emily, Cassie turns her head. Eppler comes to the table.*

EPPLER: The police are in control, Mr. Hazen. Everything is all right.

ALEX: Why the hell weren't they in control before anything happened? It's the second time in a week.

HALSEY: Good-by, Mrs. Hazen.

ALEX: It's beginning to look as if the police don't want to be in control. All right, Halsey. *Alex moves off. Halsey bows to Emily and Cassie, moves off.*

EPPLER: How do you do, Mrs. Hazen. I will be back in a minute for your order. Excuse me. *He moves away.*

EMILY *points to Eppler:* They all seem like figures in a dream. And a dream I don't understand. None of it. Berlin's an awful place to be. You always hated it. Even when we came as little girls.

CASSIE *laughs, warmly:* Remember how the horn on the Kaiser's automobile used to play the horn call from *Siegfried* and how angry it always made your father? And once —we must have been about ten—you said you thought it was pretty and why didn't you have an automobile like that? I thought your father was going to kill you. How is he?

EMILY: He's fine. I haven't seen him for six or seven months. He came over for the wedding, of course, and— *Stops.* Alex and I wrote you about the wedding. You never answered us.

CASSIE: I wrote to Alex.

EMILY *after a second:* Yes? Why not to me?

CASSIE: Because I thought it was between Alex and me. Not for the three of us.

EMILY *slowly:* What did Alex think?

CASSIE: I don't know. He wrote back he hoped we would all meet soon and that he thought you missed me.

EMILY *slowly:* I do miss you.

CASSIE: Strange that Alex didn't tell you we had written to each other. Don't you talk about things like that?

EMILY *carefully:* Things like what?

CASSIE: Like me.

EMILY *softly:* You haven't been a problem, Cassie.

CASSIE *laughs:* I feel dismissed. And I don't believe you.

EMILY *looks up at her, thoughtfully:* I know what's happening to you and me. We want to talk about ourselves, and we're frightened to. So we're ending up with the kind of talk that an hour from now neither of us will be sure we understood. So let's really talk, or let's quit.

CASSIE: I said I didn't believe you.

EMILY *quickly:* Cassie, I don't want to hurt you—

CASSIE *sharply:* And I don't want you to patronize me by trying not to.

EMILY: I'm not doing that, Cassie.

CASSIE *touches her hand:* All right, Em. I'm upset today and—

EMILY: I know. I am, too. This is a bad place to be. I'd like to go back home for a few months. I don't want to have the baby here.

CASSIE: When are you going to have the baby?

EMILY: March.

CASSIE: You always said you didn't think people should have babies so soon after they were married. That they should wait and find out if the marriage was going to work out—

EMILY: This marriage has worked out very well.

CASSIE: You're very sure about it, aren't you? What did Alex tell you when he came back from seeing me? When he came back to Rome where you were waiting for him?

EMILY: I didn't make you and Alex fight. I didn't even know you'd had a fight for months after he came back to Rome. Then all he ever told me was that you disagreed with what he thought and what he was, and that you'd both decided to quit. What good is this, Cassie? It's all over with now.

CASSIE: Is it, Em? Is it really? Your best friend marries your beau and a year after it's as if it never happened. You've always done that, Em. You've always made things as simple as you wanted them to be.

EMILY: Your best friend married your beau. But only after you'd given him up, and Alex told me it was finished for him. You won't make me feel guilty about that now or ever. You and Alex would have been very wrong for each other and I think you know it. Alex and I have a happy marriage and— Why are you in Berlin? Why are you here? *Looks up, sees Cassie looking at her. Sharply:* Why are you in Berlin? Why are you here?

CASSIE *shrugs:* I worked hard at college last year and I wanted a vacation. *Quickly:* I wanted to see you and Alex. I wanted to find out if we could be as good friends as we used to be. But all that was pretty fancy because I seemed to have been the only one who was disturbed. And now that's all right, I think, and we can—

EMILY: I don't believe it's all right now. Things are very wrong between us. Cassie, let's not dine tonight. Let's not—

CASSIE *softly:* Let's not see each other again. That's right. But it isn't easy to put away the people you've loved and been close to—

EMILY *touches Cassie's hand:* It isn't easy for me, either. But it doesn't have to be for always. We'll forget after a while. You'll get married and have children and we'll rock on the porch of a summer hotel and watch our kids play together and laugh that it could ever have been any other way—

CASSIE *very sharply:* Please. Please. Please stop talking that way.

EMILY *stares at her, then after a second:* Good-by, Cas. *As she begins to rise,*

CURTAIN FALLS

Act Two: Scene 2

The living room of a large suite in the Hotel Meurice, Paris, 1938. It is a large room with the usual French hotel furniture. Upstage, right, is a door leading to a bedroom. Upstage, left, is a door leading to the hall of the apartment. Center stage, right, is a door leading into a small anteroom which is used as a waiting room for visitors. There is a large desk in one corner of the room.

James Sears, a thin, tired-looking man of fifty, is sitting at the desk. Near him is a typewriter. On the desk are many papers, long report sheets, a brief case, a small file. As the curtain rises, Sears is clipping items from a newspaper. The phone rings.

SEARS *picks up the phone:* Hello. Could I take a message? This is James Sears, Ambassador Hazen's secretary. Hold on. Perhaps I can reach him now. *He crosses to upstage right door, knocks, opens the door:* Mr. Hazen. It's the German Embassy again. Could you see the Count— *He steps back as Alex comes into the room. It is 1938 and Alex is about forty-three.* —Count Max von Stammer who— *carefully*—happens to be in Paris and would like to drop in?

ALEX: Yes, I know he "happens" to be here. All right. Make clear it's an informal call, I just "happen" to be in

Paris, et cetera. *As Sears turns to phone, Alex picks up a clip of papers.*

SEARS: His Excellency will be glad to see Count von Stammer if he can be here within the next half hour. We're at the Hotel Meurice. You understand we are not receiving official visitors. The Ambassador is in Paris on a vacation. Yes, I will explain. Thank you. *Hangs up, turns to Alex:* Count von Stammer will be making a "social" call. He, too, is only in Paris on a vacation, and—

ALEX: All right. You both got that nonsense on the record. *Holds out the clippings.* Did Halsey get anything? Anything new here?

SEARS *takes the clippings:* The children will be evacuated from Paris tomorrow; people who can afford it are leaving for the South of France, and the railroads are dangerously clogged; there are an estimated seventy-two anti-aircraft batteries around Paris, but Halsey says he doesn't believe it. Yesterday morning, Beneš telephoned London. There's the report, supposedly compiled by the Poles, with the figures on the Soviet Union war potential. The report says Russia is in no shape to fight Germany.

ALEX: That report is two months old. Why has it appeared again?

SEARS: I asked the same question and Halsey didn't know.

ALEX *irritably:* God knows, we're not a nation of spies. Usually that pleases me. But this month it doesn't. Halsey never knows anything until the French and English have decided to give it to the Rumanians, and that's the last stop on the road to misinformation. Get Halsey. Get him on the phone for me— *Sears picks up the phone.* Never mind. Never mind. I can't make sense out of any of it, and I'm trying to blame it on him.

SEARS: I've made you a calendar, sir— I don't think you'll need Halsey—

ALEX: Washington must think I'm dead. My report should have been sent five days ago— *Looks up.* All right. Let's hear the calendar. Dates, at least, are facts.

SEARS *takes a sheet of paper from the desk:* Two weeks ago Bonnet went to Geneva to see Litvinov. Halsey says it's true that Litvinov promised aid to Czechoslovakia and sent Bonnet to see if the Rumanians would consent to let the Russians cross the borders and go through. Three days later Bonnet, when he reported to the French Cabinet, said that Litvinov had *not* been that definite. Halsey is positive Bonnet was lying because—

ALEX: That's bright of Halsey; the one fact we have, maybe the one fact in all of Europe, is that Bonnet has never yet told the truth.

SEARS: Four days ago, Litvinov told the League of Nations that Russia will support France if she goes to the aid of Czechoslovakia, and strongly hinted she may do so even if France does not go to Czechoslovakia's aid—

ALEX: So once more out trots the supposed Polish report to discredit the quality of the Russian army. I understand. And so would a child of four.

SEARS: The rumor about the Munich meeting is still going the rounds. Halsey hasn't got anything new on it, but Halsey thinks—

ALEX: I don't want to hear one more word of what Halsey thinks. *He lies down on the couch.* What's the matter with me, Jim? Am I just tired? I can't put the pieces together, or maybe I don't want to. I don't know. I can't believe in villainy. I can't. I always want to laugh when somebody else believes in it.

The door opens and Emily, in a tailored afternoon suit, comes in. It is 1938 and Emily is about thirty-seven.

EMILY *as she comes in:* Have you seen the children, Jim?

SEARS *nods, moves toward the door:* The last I saw of Sarah, Mademoiselle was dragging her to some art gallery. Sam and Mr. Taney went for a walk. *He exits.*

EMILY *laughs:* We come to Paris every summer to meet the children. Then Father arrives and that's the last we see of Sam.

ALEX: I'm used to that. He says he's educating Sam.

EMILY: You look tired, Alex. This hasn't been much of a vacation for you. Come along to the opera tonight. They're doing *Figaro* and you like it. *Quickly:* Cassie Bowman is coming for tea. She's here this summer. I called her yesterday— *Begins to speak very quickly as if she were embarrassed.* Of course, you had lunch with her last summer, and I think the summer before, wasn't it, but I haven't seen her since 1923, I suppose—

ALEX: I've seen her this trip. I saw her last week.

EMILY *slowly:* I know. Maggie Taylor told me. I suppose you'd forgotten to tell me—

ALEX: She called here one evening. You were out somewhere, and we had a late dinner together.

EMILY *pleasantly:* Yes. I'm sure you forgot to tell me—

ALEX: Oh, only half forgot, I suppose. I've never understood about you and Cassie. She's here every summer, usually when we are. I don't understand why you don't want to see each other— Or, for that matter, why it's important one way or the other.

EMILY *slowly:* I don't know either. *Then hesitantly:* But I think after all these years, I'd like to see her alone.

ALEX *pleasantly:* Of course.

EMILY *as she reaches the door, suddenly, warmly:* Come and take a walk with me, Alex. I haven't really seen you for days. It's warm and pleasant out and we'll find a quiet street where nobody's selling papers or flying south or talking about war—

ALEX: Thank you, Em. I can't. I've got people coming.

EMILY: All right. I'll be back. *She exits. As she exits, the door leading to the anteroom opens and Sears comes in.*

SEARS: He's here. You want him in now? *Alex nods, rises. Sears opens the door:* Count von Stammer. *A very old man comes in from the anteroom.*

VON STAMMER: The last time I saw you was at the Conference in Genoa in 1922. Your wife's father was with you. A remarkable man, Mr. Taney. Is he dead? How do you do?

ALEX: No, sir. He's very much alive. *They shake hands.* He's here now. He comes to Europe every year to see our children.

VON STAMMER *sits down near the desk. He is a calm man and he does not move during the scene:* I thought he died. When you get my age you want people to die. My apologies to Mr. Taney. Is he still, in politics, a great liberal?

ALEX: Mr. Taney retired many years ago.

VON STAMMER *giggles:* All liberals retired with the Versailles Treaty. *Leans down, strokes Alex's brief case.* I like leather. I have never had for myself a brief case. Next year I buy one. *Pats it.* Expensive?

ALEX *smiles:* I don't remember.

VON STAMMER: That is interesting: not to remember how much something costs. Now. The truth is, Your Excellency, I have made the journey from Berlin to see you. It was considered best to send such as me to see a man such as you. Otherwise, Von Ribbentrop would have come himself.

ALEX: I don't know Von Ribbentrop.

VON STAMMER: You should. An able man. It is the grand style to laugh at those who sold champagne, but that is not sensible.

ALEX: I don't find him laughed at. I am told he is a great social success here and in London.

VON STAMMER: Those people. They take up anybody.

ALEX *carefully:* Yes. Homosexuals one year and Nazis the next.

VON STAMMER *giggles:* And one year they combine both, eh? *Gaily:* Well, now. I have come to influence you. The French and British and Russians and Poles will also send, eh? Ach, I have little faith in men influencing other men. Each of us goes the way he goes, and that way is decided early in a man's life. I have read a little Freud. *Carefully, as if to a child:* Sigmund Freud, the Jewish Viennese psychiatric physician.

ALEX *smiles:* I know his name. We have a few printing presses in America now. Now, Count von Stammer, what have you come to influence me about, and why me?

VON STAMMER: I come to influence you about a war, and I come to *you* because you are about to send back a report to your government.

ALEX: Your Intelligence Department is remarkable. My report is not yet written, and there are none who know about it.

VON STAMMER: There was a long discussion of you and your report at a dinner party last night. By ten o'clock this morning, Mr. Kupczynski, the Polish Ambassador, having roused himself from his customary night of drinking, reported it to us. That meant the telephone was occupied, and so Monsieur Melchior de Polignac, he is a friend of yours—or your wife's perhaps?—was kept waiting because he, too, wished to tell us.

ALEX *after a second:* I have never met him. My wife knows him but— *Looks at his watch, sharply:* Now, Count von Stammer, I am afraid—

VON STAMMER: Yes, yes. Everybody becomes bored with me in time. A great many men are bores when they grow old. Not so for me. I was always a bore.

ALEX *politely:* I remember my father spoke of you.

VON STAMMER *laughs:* Now. So. Quickly. Hitler wishes the Sudetenland. He is convinced it belongs to the German Reich. The British and French will come to agree with him. With some reluctance, perhaps—

ALEX *stares at him. After a pause:* I do not believe that. *Points to the window:* The streets are filled with men being called up. People are being evacuated from Paris. Those are not the signs of people who wish—

VON STAMMER: I did not say *people* wished. I said the governments do not want a war, and they will not fight a war. The mobilization is to frighten the *people* out of a war. *Sharply:* Your Excellency, I do not have to tell you that. You know it.

ALEX: Then, perhaps, you will tell me what I don't know.

VON STAMMER: What I have to say is most simple: we would like to know that your government will not bring pressure on England or France to make war with us.

ALEX *sharply:* It is your country which is making the demands, it is your country which is trying to make war. Now, Count von Stammer, if you have come here to get assurances from me, your visit is wasted. I don't make the policy of my country. No one man makes it, thank God. And I am an unimportant man sending back an unimportant report.

VON STAMMER: No report is unimportant to my new bosses. *Smiles, as Alex is about to speak:* Let us go back, Your Excellency. You have said that my country wishes to make war. That is a large generality. Let us put it this way: what war, with whom—and when? Not over the Sudetenland. Hitler has promised that if the Sudetenland is ceded, there will be no further attempt—

ALEX: What war, with whom—and when?

VON STAMMER: I speak unofficially, of course. But if we are given the proper freedom and co-operation we might be prepared, in time, to turn East. East. To rid Europe of the menace of Russia. We realize you would wish such a promise to come from men more highly placed than I. So I have been instructed to suggest to you—

ALEX *gets up:* I am an old-fashioned man. After all these years in Europe, my roots are still deep in America. Therefore, I don't like such promises or such deals, and I do not believe they will be considered by *any* other democracy. I resent the deals of war, and I don't like your coming here with them.

VON STAMMER *looks up, puzzled, amused:* Well. Well. I have always admired Americans. If they eat dinner with a man, he must be honorable. If they ride with the Esterhazys in Hungary and the Potockis in Poland, they must be honorable men. How could men who dine out, or mount horses, be otherwise?

ALEX: I do not ride and I seldom dine out.

VON STAMMER *rises:* Ambassador Hazen, encourage the English and French not to make war. They are now willing to give us—

ALEX *quickly:* I know of nothing they are willing to give you. I know of no decision they have made. *Rings the bell on the desk.* And now I hope you will excuse me. I have an appointment.

VON STAMMER: You know of no decision they have made? Is it possible? Well. By the end of this week I would guess that a journey will be made and a conference will be held. And if there is no meddling from your side of the world, all will be settled. And if your side of the world does meddle, I would guess that— *Shrugs.* Well—it will still be settled. *Sears enters.* You look worried. Do not worry. Peace may come this year, but war will come another. Naturally, I speak this afternoon as if I thought it is wise to be on the side of my country. But I do not always think that. And I do not much care. In two months I buy a house in Switzerland. And a brief case. I have had an undistinguished career, but I might like to write about it. I cannot be more foolish than the rest. *He puts out his hand. They shake hands. The Count exits, Sears closes the door, exits.*

ALEX *picks up the phone:* Vaugirard 1209. Please. *After a second:* This is Alex Hazen. Is Halsey there? Put him on. Halsey? Von Stammer was just here. He's hinting they've reached a decision. Has there been any news? All right. Call me. *He hangs up. After a second, there is a knock on the hall door. Alex ignores it. A second later there is another knock. Irritably:* Come in, come in. *Cassie comes in. Cassie is thirty-seven years old. She has on a simple afternoon dress.*

CASSIE *stands looking at him:* You sound so irritable. I'll go away.

ALEX *turns, smiles:* I'm sorry, my dear. Come in. How are you?

CASSIE: You didn't phone to find out. But they were wonderful flowers, and I thank you for them.

ALEX: I wouldn't have been any fun to be with. I've had a miserable week. I've got to send back a report and I—

CASSIE: Haven't you sent off that report? You mentioned it when we dined last week.

ALEX: No, I haven't sent it off. I've been stalling. I don't know what's the matter with me. I've never gone in for thinking about myself. Sometimes I've been right and when I was wrong I always thought, well, you've done your best; you can't sit around and cry about mistakes. Everybody makes them. But now—

CASSIE *gently*: But now what?

ALEX: One minute I say to myself, what difference does it make what you write back? It'll be one of many reports coming in this week. But that's not true because I've got to do my best, even if it isn't important to anybody but me—

CASSIE: Then do your best.

ALEX *wearily*: The truth is I don't know what's best.

CASSIE *gently*: Back doing business at the old stand, Alex?

ALEX *looks up at her*: A German just left here who remembered me at the Genoa Conference. When he said it, that time in Rome, and you and me, came back so sharply that I could have cried. *Gets up, turns away.* I don't know why.

CASSIE *after a second*: Why did Emily ask me here today?

ALEX: I don't know. I suppose she wants to see you again.

CASSIE: Does she know I saw you last week?

ALEX: Yes, I told her. But she knew it. Maggie Taylor had told her. I'm not sure how Maggie knew but— *Looks at his watch.* Emily's late. I hope there wasn't trouble in the streets. She's never late.

CASSIE: Did she mind your seeing me?

ALEX: She knows I've seen you each summer. Why should she mind? *Shrugs.* You and she haven't wanted to see each other; you and I have.

CASSIE *softly:* That simple? That simple for her, too?

ALEX: Isn't it simple? Is there anything wrong with it?

CASSIE: You've been a faithful husband and pure in heart. *Suddenly gets up.* I must go now. Tell Em I couldn't wait.

ALEX: I'll be finished work tonight. How about lunch tomorrow? I'll drive you into the country—

CASSIE: I'm sorry. I can't.

ALEX: How about dinner? *She shakes her head.* But I want to see you. It will be a whole year again—

CASSIE: I don't think I'll be coming next year. Things are getting too expensive for a teacher's vacation. The world is cracking up, my dear; I don't think anybody will be coming.

ALEX *catches her arm:* I want a day off. Spend it with me. I'll buy you flowers and—

CASSIE *laughs:* No. I'm going to Fontainebleau for a week. Remember that little hotel we used to go to when we were kids? I still go back every year.

ALEX *quickly:* Have you a beau, Cassie?

CASSIE *after a second:* A half beau, I guess.

ALEX: Why haven't you ever got married?

CASSIE: Maybe I don't marry easy. Maybe— *Stops suddenly*. Can I ask you? *He nods*. Are you in love with Emily?

ALEX *simply:* I love Emily. Very much, I think. But I— *Takes her arm*. Oh, Cassie, it's taken me fifteen years to say these words even to myself: I was only in love once.

CASSIE *very softly:* Me, too.

ALEX *turns, takes her arms:* Let me come down to the country to see you. Please, Cas.

CASSIE *very nervously:* I—er, I want to, Alex. The truth is, I've wanted to for a long time, I mean— But I don't want it to be wrong. I—I couldn't stand it if it worried you afterwards or you felt guilty, or Emily— Or I felt guilty—

ALEX: I don't feel guilty. Emily's been a good wife. And I've been a good husband, too. I think I'll go on being. This has nothing to do with Emily. This has to do with you and me. From a long, long time ago. It's a strange day for us to come together again. Strange for me to be thinking about myself and you when— *He puts his arms around her*. Please, Cas. Let me come down.

CASSIE *looks up at him. After a second, smiles:* All right, darling. It will make me happy. I hope it will make you happy, too. *She touches his face, then moves away*. I'll go now. Tell Em I couldn't wait. And tell her I don't want to come again.

ALEX *frowns:* Cas, I want no more talk of Emily. Yes? *He leans down to kiss her*. Good-by, darling. I'll be down. *She smiles, exits*.

ALEX *goes to the desk, sits down, picks up clippings. After a second, he puts his hand over his face, as if he were very tired. Then he goes back to the clippings, begins to read them. Suddenly he leans back, speaks sharply:* Jim, what is this? This clipping about Mrs. Hazen? What paper does it come from? Why don't you mark the papers?— It's a pretty item all right. Jim! Where are you?— *Turns around, sees that Sears is not in the anteroom, slams the door. The hall door opens and Emily comes slowly in. She is carrying packages.*

EMILY *nervous and speaking rapidly:* I never saw so many cars in my life. Everybody is leaving Paris. They don't believe there's going to be a war, but they are leaving just in case.

ALEX: Cassie was here.

EMILY: I don't understand them. If we were at war and Washington or New York were in danger, I wouldn't leave. It's your country; you just don't pack up and go when there's trouble.

ALEX *looks at her:* I am glad to hear that.

EMILY *after a second:* You're upset today, Alex.

ALEX *picks up the clipping:* You've been seeing too much of the Renaults and Melchior de Polignac and the fashionable society trash who run with them. I don't like these gossip items of you with people like that. These are sharp times, Emily, and where one went to dinner a few years ago, one can't go any longer.

EMILY *sits down:* I've been lonely, Alex, for a long time. I see the people who come along. Sometimes I like them, sometimes I don't. They don't mean much to me one way or the other.

ALEX: Everybody thinks that about the people they see. And it's never really true. I'm sorry you've been lonely, Em. I guess I have been, too. Cas was here.

EMILY *very quickly:* Are you coming to the opera with us?

ALEX: No, I'm going to do the report. I've got to get to work now.

EMILY: Oh, I'm sorry you're not coming. I'd looked forward to it. But I am glad you're going to do the report. It's been worrying you so much. *Slowly:* It's an important report. You're a sound man and you will be listened to. It comes down to peace or war now, doesn't it? Last night at dinner Toni said the Czechs were acting like fools. He said if Hitler got what he wanted now that would shut him up for good. And Baudouin said if there is war it means Russia in Europe and—

ALEX *sharply:* That's what I meant. That kind of people and that kind of talk. Toni has been doing business with the Nazis for years and Baudouin's bank is tied up with the Japs.

EMILY *slowly:* I have a lot of investments in his bank. They've been there since my grandfather.

ALEX *looks at her:* That's bad news. I've never known about your money. *Slowly:* Why are you telling me now, Em?

EMILY: You've made a great point of not knowing about my money, and not touching it. I wonder if you were scared to find out we are rich; to find out we are the people we are.

ALEX *comes over to her:* You've never talked about your money before. I don't know what you mean now. But if I thought you were trying to tell me that what I think or believe or will report should be influenced by it, I would be very angry, Em. Very angry with both of us.

EMILY: I don't mean to influence you with my money. I have it, I'm glad to have it, and it's never meant much to me. But I'm not willing to lie to myself about money, or where and how I was born, or the world I've lived in. But sometimes I think you pretend to yourself that you have no world that influences you—that you have no connections and no prejudices. Why don't you try to see that they all have something to do with you? Maybe it isn't all on the basis of honor.

ALEX: I've always tried to push aside what I am, or where your money is, or how we live, and see what's best for my country. I've tried to do that. *Sharply:* I'm going to keep on trying.

EMILY *slowly:* Can you push aside your son?

ALEX: What's Sam got to do with this?

EMILY *slowly, carefully:* If there is a war, he'll soon be old enough to fight in it. *Tensely:* I don't want my son to die. I don't want you to have anything to do with his dying. I don't like Nazis any better than you do. But I don't want a war. I love Sam, and I want him to be happy, in a peaceful world.

ALEX *very sharply:* I love Sam too. But I'll report what I

think is the truth. And it will have nothing to do with my desire to keep Sam alive. I fought in a war and I wouldn't have wanted my father— *Desperately:* What are we saying to each other? We've never had fights, we've never talked to each other this way.

EMILY *softly:* You and I haven't been close to each other for a long time.

ALEX: I know. I've been lonely and so have you. This afternoon I suddenly knew it—Cassie was here, Em, and—

EMILY *very quickly:* I know, Alex. You've told me that three times before. I saw her. I was in the lobby. I waited for her to leave. I didn't want to see her. It sounds crazy, but I was kind of afraid to come up—

ALEX: Afraid to see Cassie? What are you talking about? You asked her here— *Looks at her.* I never thought you were afraid of anything.

EMILY: I'm going to tell you about me—some day when we're very old and you're so deaf you can't hear me. I am afraid of a great many things. Including—

The anteroom door opens and Sears puts his head in.

SEARS *tensely:* There's an announcement from London. On the radio. *As Alex moves swiftly to the radio, Sears goes out, closes the door.*

RADIO: The announcement has just been made that Prime Minister Chamberlain and Premier Daladier will fly to Munich tomorrow morning. There are already hints of Cabinet resignations. Although no official statement, other than the announcement of an hour ago, has been forthcoming, a high official source said a few minutes ago that—

ALEX *snaps off the radio. After a second:* Well, there's your peace.

EMILY: Does that mean they will give him the Sudeten?

ALEX: Yes, of course.

EMILY: I'm sorry for that. I thought maybe they'd find another way— Oh, I don't know what I thought. *Sharply:* Why did you call it *my* peace? I didn't want anybody to suffer—

ALEX *sharply:* No, of course. Nobody wants anybody to suffer. Maybe even that decadent trash in the society columns don't want it.

EMILY *coming to him, tensely, angrily:* If it makes you feel better to make fun of those people, then do it. But don't tell yourself that having contempt for them puts you on the opposite side. Why are you attacking me, and unjustly, I think?

ALEX: I suppose I am being unjust. I think I even know why.

EMILY: Oh.

ALEX: I don't know how to tell you, Em, but maybe it is a good day to get things straight—

EMILY *quickly:* I think we've talked enough, Alex. Sometimes putting things in words makes them too definite, before one really means them to be. You're having a hard time. *Looks toward the window.* It's as if a machine were running us all down and we didn't know where to go or what to do or how to get away from it. *Turns away. After a second:* Shall I call Sears for you? *He nods. She moves to-*

ward the anteroom door. All right, Jim. The Ambassador's ready. I'll have them send up food for you and Jim. Good night, darling.

ALEX *softly:* Good night, Em.

Emily exits. As she exits the anteroom door opens and Sears comes in. He goes to the typewriter, sits down, waits.

SEARS *after a second:* All ready, sir. Shall I take it straight on the machine?

ALEX: No. Yes. Take it any way you want. *Lies down on the couch. After a second:* "By the time this reaches you the results of the Munich meeting will be known. But there is no doubt here that the Sudeten will be given to Germany in return for the promise that it will be the last of Hitler's demands. That I do not believe." *Pause. Begins to dictate again:* "I have been told by Count Max von Stammer that the agreement will probably carry a second promise: Hitler will talk of making war at some time in the future on the Soviet Union. That I do not believe, although it has long been a rumor here. It is my earnest recommendation— *Alex gets up, moves toward the typewriter.* "It is my belief—"

SEARS: "Earnest recommendation."

ALEX: What the hell has one man got to do with history? There's something crazy about sitting here and thinking that what I say makes any difference. What do I know? What does anybody know? What the hell could they do at home, anyway? All right. "Earnest belief that we should protest against any further German aggressions or against any further concessions to them. But I am convinced that

Mr. Chamberlain is working in the interests of peace and his actions must not be judged too sharply. If he can save his sons and our sons from war—" *Stops suddenly.* Take out that last. *Sits down.* "It is difficult to give you a picture of a muddled situation. On the side of peace there are many selfish and unpatriotic men willing to sacrifice the honor of their country for their own private and dishonorable reasons, and of those who deplore the Munich meeting—and I am one of them—many see it as a complete capitulation and as the beginning of a world war. I think that is a harsh and unwarranted judgment based on inadequate facts. If a generation can be kept from war, if we can spare our sons—" Take out that last sentence. *Looks up at Sears as if he were frightened. Then, violently:* All right. Code it and send it as a cable.

The door opens and Moses comes in. He is in dinner clothes, but without a tie.

ALEX: How many drinks does it take to get drunk? I haven't been drunk in twenty years— *He looks up at Moses, annoyed, goes on speaking to Sears:* Finish it and let's go out and get drunk and forget about it for a few hours.

MOSES: Really? Drunk? I shall wait up to see you. Ah, I shouldn't interrupt the master work. So the news is all in? The boys are going to Munich. Well, I'll be glad to sail home and get back to my chair in the library. We may be crooks at home, but we aren't elegant about it. I can't stand elegant crooks. They talk too pious for me.

ALEX *wearily:* Whatever I feel about them, or you feel about them, maybe they're acting for the best. It can't be easy to throw your country into a war.

MOSES: What a simple way of putting it, and how understanding you are. I feel sorry for people who are as tolerant as you.

ALEX *gets up, moves toward his room. Slowly, angrily:* Thank you. I find I'm sorry for myself. *Exits.*

MOSES *to Sears*: Mrs. Hazen is making me go to the opera. I need a tie. Ask the Ambassador to lend me one, will you? I hate the opera. There's something insane about people opening their mouths very wide. What's the Ambassador saying in his report, Jim?

SEARS: I'm a confidential secretary, Mr. Taney.

MOSES: Good for you. *As Sears crosses the room:* As usual, Sophronia has packed everything.

Sears exits. Moses goes to the desk, picks up the report, stands reading it. After a second, Sears reappears carrying a black tie. He stares at Moses.

SEARS: For God's sake, Mr. Taney. That's official. Since when do people read other people's?—

MOSES: Since when do people read other people's mail? Since always.

SEARS: I—I—

Moses takes the tie, waves Sears aside, moves to Alex's door.

MOSES *calls in:* Difficult world, eh, Alex? So many men doing so many strange things. All we can do is compromise. Compromise and compromise. There's nothing like a good compromise to cost a few million men their lives.

Well, I'm glad I retired. I don't like having anything to do with the death of other people. Sad world, eh, Alex? *The door slams. Moses smiles.* Very sad.

CURTAIN FALLS

Act Two: Scene 3

The drawing room of the Hazen house about an hour after Scene III of Act I.
Cassie is sitting on the couch. Emily is sitting near her. Alex is standing near the fireplace. Moses is sitting on the terrace, staring into the room. Sam is standing in the doorway.

CASSIE *after a long silence:* Well, Emily. Are we finished?

EMILY *quietly:* Do you remember one summer Father took us to Fontainebleau and left us for a week with Sophronia? We rented bicycles—

Sam closes the terrace doors, disappears.

EMILY *waits, begins to speak:* And the first hour we had them, I fell down that steep hill and the rest of the week Sophronia made us play on the porch of the hotel so she could watch us— *Turns to Cassie, slowly:* Why did you go back to *that* hotel the week-end that you and Alex first?—

ALEX: For God's sake, Emily. If you'd wanted to know about me and Cassie, I would have told you. Did we have to go through all the fumblings, all the mistakes of years, to find it out? Like everybody else in the world, I don't want to look back on what was wrong—

CASSIE *with great force:* None of us. None of us. It hasn't been a pretty picture. *To Emily:* And not of you, either.

EMILY: That's true. I haven't liked myself in it. I haven't liked myself for a long time now. *To Alex:* I knew about you and Cassie. I've known about you and Cassie for—

CASSIE: Then why did you do this? And why tonight?

EMILY: Tonight has been coming for a long time. When I found out you were here in Washington I knew that now we'd have to meet and get it finished. Always it's been the three of us, all our lives. We can't go on that way.

CASSIE *softly:* That's right. That's right.

EMILY *coming to Cassie, with great emotion:* Let's get it straight, Cassie. Because if we don't we'll pay hard for it. Do it now. Not only for me. Not only for Alex. For yourself. It's time to tell the truth. Please, Cassie. Please.

CASSIE: I know, I know. *Softly:* In a minute, Em. *After a second she slowly gets up, goes to Alex, stands next to him, speaks nervously, haltingly. Emily walks across the room as if to move away from them.* You know, when you don't think you're bad, then you have a hard time seeing you did things for a bad reason, and you fool yourself that way. You don't do anything for just one reason. It gets all mixed up and—maybe the hardest thing in the world is to see yourself straight. The truth is, I was haunted by Emily, all my life. You always said I talked too much about Emily and asked too many questions. I was angry when Emily married you—I felt it had been done against me. I had no plans then to do anything about it but— *To Alex, swiftly, desperately:* I wanted to take you away from Emily; there it is. It sounds as if I didn't care about you, but I did and I do. But I would never have done anything about you if I hadn't wanted, for so many years, to punish Emily—

I didn't know that was true until tonight. *Puts her hands to her face:* That's a lie. I did know it. But I never wanted to see it. I don't want to see it now— I— *Alex takes her hand from her face, holds her hand.* I think I used to be worth something. But this got in the way of everything: my work, other people. Well, I guess you pay for small purposes, and for bitterness. *Turns to Alex, touches his hand.* I can't say I'm sorry. I can say I got mixed up and couldn't help myself. *Pauses, turns slowly to look at Emily.* I've always envied you, Emily. Your life seemed so full and your world so exciting. But if I learned about myself tonight, I also learned about you. And you, Alex. It's too bad that all these years I saw us wrong— *With great feeling:* Oh, I don't want to see another generation of people like us who didn't know what they were doing or why they did it. You know something? We were frivolous people. All three of us, and all those like us— Tell your son to try— *After a second.* Good-by, my dear.

ALEX *gets up, softly:* Good-by, Cassie. *He takes her hand. She smiles. Then she moves to Emily.*

CASSIE: Somebody told me once that when something's been wrong with you and it gets cured, you miss it very much, at first. *Warmly:* I'm going to miss you, in a funny kind of way.

EMILY *warmly:* Good-by, Cas. *She presses Cassie's arm. Cassie moves swiftly into the hall, disappears. After a second, Emily speaks warmly and affectionately:* You feel bad. I'm sorry.

ALEX: *You* feel bad and *I'm* sorry and what good does it

do? *Pauses.* Em, unless you want to, I'd like not to talk about it for a long time and then we can if—

EMILY *simply:* We don't ever have to talk about it. We'll just see how it works out.

Emily goes to the piano, starts to play. Alex turns toward the terrace, looks at Emily. He moves to the terrace doors, opens them. Sam is walking on the terrace.

ALEX *after a pause:* The doctor told you not to walk much. Why are you doing it?

SAM *as he comes into the room:* It feels good. *Quickly, to Emily:* I haven't heard you play in a long time. It's nice.

EMILY: I think I'll take lessons again.

MOSES *coming into the room:* Remarkable your liking music, Emily. It doesn't suit you.

EMILY: Do you know what suits me, Father?

MOSES *thoughtfully:* No, I suppose not.

SAM *moving to hall:* Well, good night. I—

ALEX: Sam, don't pretend nothing's happened tonight. We'll all be better off if you don't do it that way. If you have anything to say, say it.

SAM: There was a lot I didn't understand tonight, and a lot that isn't any of my business. But there is— Never mind. Some other night.

EMILY *gets up from the piano:* We've seen a good deal of you the last few months, and your father and I sensed that things were worrying you, many things, some of them about us. We didn't want you here tonight; it was hard for us to take. But when you wanted to stay, I thought we owed it to you. You're not doing us a favor now by sparing us what you think.

SAM *turns to Alex:* All right. That day before Munich, in your report, did you really—*Haltingly*—recommend appeasement?

ALEX: I didn't know that word then but that's what it came down to.

EMILY: I had a lot to do with it, Sam.

SAM: I know.

MOSES *moves toward Sam:* Look here. There've been many times when I haven't agreed with your father. But you mustn't blame him too much. What he or anybody else recommended wouldn't have made any difference.

SAM *to Moses:* History is made by the masses of people. One man, or ten men, don't start the earthquakes and don't stop them either. Only hero worshipers and ignorant historians think they do. You wrote me that in a letter once. You said it was what Tolstoi meant in *War and Peace.*

MOSES: And I hope you still agree with it.

SAM: I do, I do. But you've made it an excuse to just sit back and watch; nothing anybody can do makes any difference, so why do it?

ALEX: That isn't what Tolstoi meant. It's only what your grandfather wanted him to mean. At least I never kidded myself that way.

SAM *turns to Moses, smiles:* I think you mixed me up quite a lot, Grandpa. *Quickly, as Moses is about to speak:* But one fine thing you taught me: that I belong here. I never liked that school in France or the one in Switzerland. I didn't like being there.

EMILY: You should have told us.

SAM: I wouldn't have known how to say it. *Smiles.* You know, I never felt at home any place until I got in the army. I never came across my kind of people until I met Leck and Davis. *Quickly:* I guess I never could have belonged to your world nor to Grandpa's, either— I still don't know where I do belong. I guess that's what's been worrying me. But with only one leg you've got to start thinking faster— *Gets up quickly, as if he were startled by what he'd said. Emily gets up; Alex moves toward Sam; Moses turns sharply. Sam looks around as if he were panic-stricken. Then he speaks quickly:* I have to go back to the hospital tomorrow night. They've decided it's something called traumatic sarcoma of the bone and they can't avoid the amputation any longer. I was going to tell you tomorrow.

Alex starts to move toward Sam, stops, puts his hand over his face.

EMILY *very softly:* Sam, Sam.

MOSES *after a long pause:* I guess I'll go to bed. *As he moves toward Sam, he begins to cry.* I hope you won't laugh at me but I would have given my life if I could have saved you any— *Without looking at Sam, he touches his arm. Sam smiles, presses Moses' arm.* Well, son. *He moves slowly to the hall door, exits.*

SAM *softly:* I'm sorry I told you tonight—

ALEX *with great feeling:* Don't be sorry for us.

EMILY *with great feeling:* I hate pity for the relatives. It's your leg. It's your trouble and nobody else will ever know anything about it. *Very loudly:* We'll be walking all right. But you won't— *She puts her hands over her face.*

SAM *sharply:* All right, Mother. *To Alex:* I was lucky. Out of nine men, four got killed. *Nervously, looking at Emily, talking as if he wanted to make conversation:* Did you tour around that part of Italy, Father? They call the place Bloody Basin now because it's a sort of basin between two hills and so many guys got killed there that we called it Bloody Basin. *Alex goes to Emily, leans down, kisses her.*

SAM *speaks chattily, as if for Emily:* I liked Leck, you know, the boy I've told you about who used to be a baker in Jersey City. We'd sit around and talk: why we were in the war, and what was going to happen afterwards, and all of us pretended we knew more than we did. But not Leck. He never pretended to anything because he really knew a lot. Sometimes they'd ask me about you, Father, and I'd tell them all the things you'd done. Then one day one of them handed me a clipping. His mother had sent it to him. *As if it were painful:* I don't think I ever in my life was really ashamed before. After all the fine talk I'd done about my family— God in Heaven, it did something to me— *Stops abruptly.*

EMILY: What is it?

SAM: Never mind.

ALEX *tensely:* Say it, Sam, say it.

SAM: I was thinking Mother had had enough and—

EMILY *sharply:* Stop being sorry for me.

SAM *takes a newspaper clipping from his pocket:* Well, this soldier wanted to make fun of me, I guess. It's from one of those women columnists. It's about a dinner party that she gave. Kind of international people were there, she says. A French novelist, and a milliner who used to be a White Russian, and a movie actress, and a banker from Holland— *Slowly begins to read from the clipping:* "It was, if I say so myself, a brilliant gathering. The last to arrive was the handsome Mrs. Alexander Hazen. Her husband, Alex Hazen, used to be our Ambassador to—"

EMILY *sharply:* Your father wasn't at the dinner.

ALEX *wearily:* That doesn't matter. Go on, Sam.

SAM *reads:* "I looked around the table and I thought, 'Europe isn't dead. These people will go home some day and once more make it the charming, careless, carefree place I knew so well.' " So the soldier who gave me the clipping says, "Glad to be sitting in mud here, Sam, if it helps to make a carefree world for your folks—" And Leck tells him to shut up. But when we're alone, Leck says to me, "Sam, that banker the piece talked about, he used to deal with the Germans before it got too hot. He's a no good guy. And the rest of those people, they're all old tripe who just live in our country now and pretend they are on the right side. When the trouble came in their countries they sold out their people and beat it quick, and now they make believe they're all for everything good. My God, Sam," he said, "if you come from that you better get away from it fast, because they helped to get us where we are."

ALEX *comes to Sam:* Sometimes I was wrong because I didn't know any better. And sometimes I was wrong because I had reasons I didn't know about. But I never had anything to do with people like that.

EMILY: Maybe I've no right to ask you. But try not to be too hard on us, Sam.

SAM *as if he hadn't heard her:* Well, for a couple of days I thought about what Leck said and I was going to tell him something. But that afternoon we went down to Bloody Basin and he got blown to pieces and I got wounded. *Looks up at Emily as if he had just heard what she said.* How do you say you love your country?

EMILY *after a second:* I don't know. We're frightened of saying things like that now because we might sound like the fakers who do say them.

SAM *gets up:* Well, I want to say it. I love this place. *With great passion:* And I don't want any more fancy fooling around with it. I don't want any more of Father's mistakes, for any reason, good or bad, or yours, Mother, because I think they do it harm. I was ashamed of that clipping. But I didn't really know why. I found out tonight. I am ashamed of both of you, and that's the truth. I don't want to be ashamed that way again. I don't like losing my leg, I don't like losing it at all. I'm scared—but everybody's welcome to it as long as it means a little something and helps to bring us out some place. All right. I've said enough. I love you both. Let's have a drink.

As Emily moves toward the table, Alex moves toward Sam.

CURTAIN FALLS